D1008319

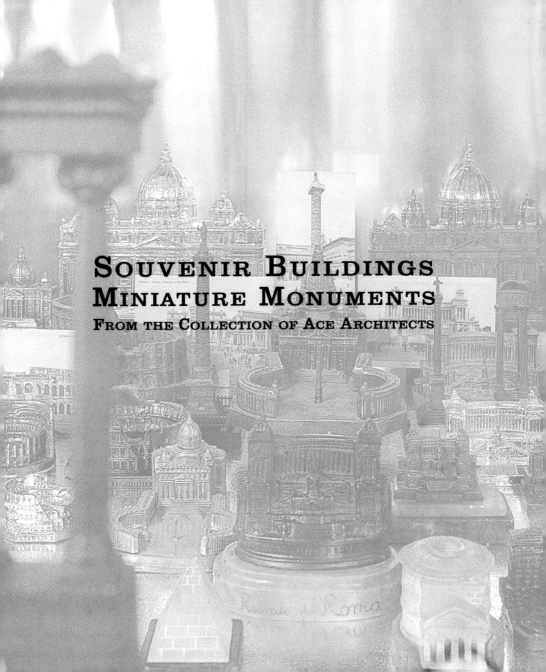

SOUVENIR BUILDINGS
MINIATURE MONUMENTS

FROM THE COLLECTION OF ACE ARCHITECTS

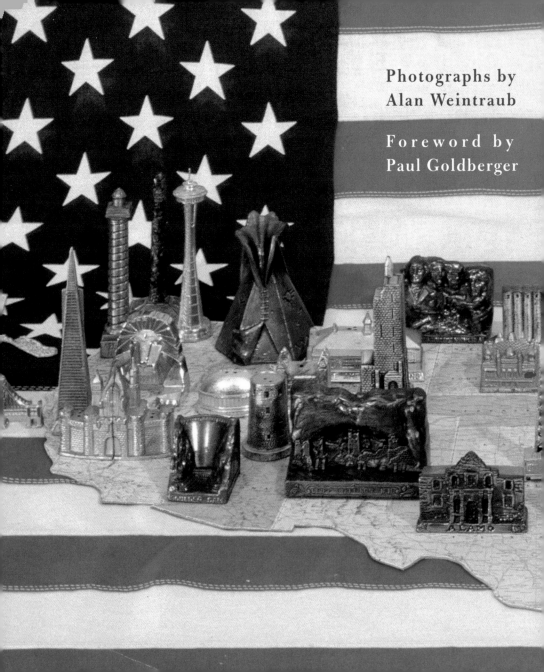

Photographs by
Alan Weintraub

Foreword by
Paul Goldberger

SOUVENIR BUILDINGS
MINIATURE MONUMENTS

FROM THE COLLECTION OF ACE ARCHITECTS
MARGARET MAJUA & DAVID WEINGARTEN

HARRY N. ABRAMS, INC., PUBLISHERS

Photographer's Dedication
FOR ALISON, NEAL, AND SCOTT.
A. J. W.

Page 1:
Rome (see page 42)

Pages 2–3:
United States monu-
ments. It's a big country
and someone's got to
build it—and so they did,
including, from left,
Hawaii's Aloha Tower, a
New Mexican cliff
dwelling, a tepee in Yel-
lowstone Park, the presi-
dential Mount Rushmore,
a Minnesotan grain eleva-
tor, Eliel Saarinen's
graceful arch signifying
the heart of the Midwest
in St. Louis, the Sears
Tower in Chicago, New
York's World Trade Cen-
ter, and the Capitol in
Washington, D.C. On the
East Coast, the Statue of
Liberty casts a welcoming
light.

EDITOR: *Ruth A. Peltason*
DESIGNER: *Darilyn Lowe Carnes*

Library of Congress Cataloging-in-Publication Data

Majua, Margaret.
    Souvenir buildings and miniature monuments : from the collection of
    Ace Architects / Margaret Majua and David Weingarten ; photographs
    by Alan Weintraub ; foreword by Paul Goldberger.
        p.   cm.
    ISBN 0–8109–4470–7 (cloth)
    1. Souvenir buildings—Private collections—California—Oakland—
Catalogs.   2. Ace Architects (Oakland, Calif.)—Art collections—
Catalogs.   I. Weingarten, David.   II. Weintraub, Alan.
    III. Title.
    NK8475.B8M35   1996
    720'.228—dc20
                                                            96–10852

Published in 1996 by Harry N. Abrams, Incorporated, New York
A Times Mirror Company

Printed and bound in China

CONTENTS

FOREWORD

SCHOLARS OF ARCHITECTURAL HISTORY, look elsewhere. Seekers of great architectural truth, pursue your mission someplace else. While David Weingarten and Margaret Majua do in this book make a momentary pass at trying to convince us that collecting miniature souvenir buildings is a serious business, I urge you to disregard it, particularly the earnest paragraphs about the way in which these tiny buildings represent "a shadow history of architecture." You know from the moment you open these pages that this book is really about something else. The real point here is what David Weingarten and Margaret Majua call "jolts of architectural essence," an absolutely wonderful phrase that in four words sums up the joyous experience that collecting, possessing, or even just seeing these miniature objects can be.

"Jolts of architectural essence"—precisely. Moments of sheer, childlike pleasure, connecting to the real world, yet somehow far away from it, too. These miniature buildings are silly, but not that silly, real, but not that real. It is the magical way in which they are poised, somewhere between the world we know and the world we make in our imaginations, that makes them so compelling. Of course all miniatures by their very nature are lovable, almost cute—anything rendered in tiny scale becomes benign, almost too sweet—but with architecture the transformation is the most striking of all. In the world of miniature souvenir buildings are great and powerful things we know and have seen a million times—the Empire State Building, say, or the Eiffel Tower—suddenly rendered toylike. The most astonishing thing is that they do not lose their power, as we might suspect; instead, they submit it to our control. The tower of St. Mark's Cathedral, the spire of the Woolworth Building, the dome of the Capitol are, in miniature, still potent symbols. But they become ours to play with, ours to maneuver like chess pieces. We take these little architectural essences and wallow in the pleasure they bring: one part nostalgia, one part power.

Plenty of people share the glorious obsession of collecting, but few have done it with the extraordinary panache of David Weingarten and Margaret Majua. It is not merely the quantity of miniature buildings they have pulled together—though at 2,400 and still growing, the size of this collection can evoke no emotion other than astonishment—or even the quality, though this collection ranks among the finest ever assembled. It is the setting that truly raises this collection to the realm of wonders, the whitewashed, wood-frame barn with its green copper-tiled roof and more than three hundred running feet of shelves inside. The "building building," as its owners like to call it, exudes an aura that is really more like the paneled library of a great house than the funky outbuilding of a ranch house in the northern California suburbs: kilim rugs, a trestle table for cataloguing work, Piranesi prints attached to the few surfaces that do not contain miniature buildings. Virtually every one of these miniature buildings is a source of pleasure in itself; put together, the effect of the whole is even more than the sum of the parts. Here is all of architecture—architecture remembered, architecture imagined, architecture invented, and architecture interpreted—turned into a realm of utter delight.

Paul Goldberger

Dedication

Large and small Speyer Cathedrals, copper-plated pot metal, 1970s

Twenty years ago, my uncle Charles Moore and I traveled together for two weeks, looking at picturesque places in Italy, Switzerland, France, and Germany. He was, by then, a famous architect. I was between sessions at architecture school.

Our route brought us to the Rhine town of Speyer, which offered the pleasures of a fine, if not famous, Romanesque cathedral. Along an aisle in this cool, dim sanctuary, nearly hidden among chapels and memorials, reposed a souvenir stand.

Perhaps I should say it was a religious articles store, for it offered a range of devotional accessories, as well as postcards, guide books, and two sizes of gold-colored miniatures of the great cathedral.

Uncle Chuck, an immoderate collector of architectural folk art and knick-knacks of every stripe, selected the large miniature for himself, while wondering at my choice of the smaller, more pathetic souvenir.

Eighteen years later, Uncle Chuck's heart finally gave out at his "spread" in Austin, Texas. In a case there, which he described as a vitrine, among a score of other souvenir buildings, resided his large miniature of the cathedral at Speyer on the Rhine.

Over those same eighteen years, my small cathedral had found its way, first, to my parents' home, and ten years ago into the fledgling collection of souvenir buildings that Margaret Majua and I had then assembled. Today, both Speyer cathedrals, apart since my Uncle Chuck's and my visit to the souvenir stand, again inhabit the same cabinet. Here they are, among the more than two thousand miniature buildings forming our collection. Who can foresee the next stopping place for these itinerant buildings?

Today I can scarcely recall that Romanesque cathedral at Speyer. Yet the two souvenir buildings provoke the most vivid recollection of that moment with my uncle.

He was right to worry over the meaning of my choice of miniatures that day. The larger souvenir is greater than its smaller relation, its detail finer and its architectural massing more powerfully rendered. Still, for me, it is the inequality of that pair of buildings, his cathedral and mine, that provides their eloquence.

Uncle Chuck's architectural enthusiasms were legion and contagious among his partners, clients, friends, students, and nephews. We all, on occasion, thrilled to see the world through his eyes. Often, those eyes were drawn to Russian Easter eggs—jeweled, Czarist confections, whose tiny interiors suggest entire realms, improbably grand and glorious.

Uncle Chuck inhabited the large world of little buildings, and was our sage guide in this place off the edge of most architectural maps. This book is dedicated to his irresistible memory.

David Weingarten
Ace Architects
Oakland, California
1996

Souvenirs and Souvenir Buildings

Along a nearly seedy stretch of Las Vegas Boulevard, halfway between the new "Las Vegas" of the Strip and the now redeveloping downtown, is an L-shaped building, wrapped around plenty of parking. A bright sign confidently proclaims this the "World's Largest Souvenir Store." The place *is* big. Moreover, the range of Las Vegas souvenirs is wide, including dozens of styles of mugs; all kinds of caps; many styles of slot machines and electronic poker keychains; ashtrays and matches; glassware; a wall of T-shirts and socks; copper jewelry; cactus plants; sunglasses; placemats, postcards, and pamphlets; scorpions and tarantulas entombed in acrylic hemispheres; rabbits' feet; refrigerator magnets; cowboy boots, beaded belts, and Westernwear; novelty items like dice clocks; ice cold beer and soda. As many as possible of these ostensibly useful items are imprinted with the words "Las Vegas," and are thereby transformed into souvenirs.

The word *souvenir* derives from the Latin *subvenire*, to come into mind; and, later, from the French for memory, *souvenir*. Horace Walpole first used souvenir in English in 1775. At the World's Largest Souvenir Store, one wonders what would appeal to Horace Walpole.

Webster's dictionary defines *souvenir* as "something kept or serving as a reminder of a place, a person, or an occasion; a keepsake; a memento." The definition of *memento* is intriguing "anything serving as a reminder, warning, or souvenir." This suggests that souvenirs may safeguard us from the perils of forgetfulness. What is the danger of failing to recall a weekend in Vegas?

In this country, whose national memory is allegedly short, the preservation of individuals' memories makes for brisk business at souvenir stands. The purchase of a souvenir is, as well, an optimistic act. It anticipates a moment in the future when the present may be worth remembering.

Of course, the many clients of the World's Largest Souvenir Store do not cart off mass quantities of mugs, T-shirts, and ashtrays with the idea of being later reminded of this store's sea of imprinted merchandise. These souvenirs are intended to provoke memories of a set of experiences of Las Vegas.

It is another variety of optimism that brings souvenir building collectors to this store. Certainly here, they believe, in this city whose colossal constructions assume every architectural form—a pyramid complete with Sphinx; castles; ancient Rome; modern skyscrapers of all types; South Seas villages; various Eastern pleasure palaces; even Paris and New York City, certainly here will be offered splendid miniature buildings. Their disappointment, our disappointment, is palpable. There are no souvenir buildings in the World's Largest Souvenir Store.

The outsized monuments of the "new" Las Vegas, and some of the more agreeably scaled old monuments, are endlessly pictured on an assortment of products. In fact, there are images of little else. Of course, these are not the same thing as actual souvenir buildings.

Souvenir buildings are, first of all, three-dimensional miniatures of actual buildings. They are almost always cast in a mold, and have been produced in a wide variety of materials, including many metals, clay, plastic, glass, plaster, shredded currency, and lately, unfortunately, resin and so-called composition. These last materials are formed into some of the least detailed, most cloddish miniatures yet seen. Souvenir buildings are likewise fashioned from sheet metal, wood and wood fibers, coal, stone, and, less enduringly, ice.

Souvenir buildings, like all souvenirs, are produced in multiples—from a precious few to thousands upon thousands upon thousands. For collectors, over-produced miniatures, even those of a stirring monument like the Empire State Building, induce a kind of queasy boredom. Singly made miniatures, such as those assembled by architects and folk artists, are less souvenirs than building models, and serve different purposes.

There are architectural miniatures whose subjects are generic, rather than actual, buildings. Often these take the form of cute houses and idealized small-town general stores, post offices, and fire stations. Most scale buildings employed in model railroad layouts are generic. By their nature, these are unrelated to specific places and are not intended to provoke any specific recollection. Generic architectural miniatures pursue aims outside of memory and, no matter how appealing, should not be thought of as souvenir buildings.

Purists extend this argument to include fairy-tale, fictional, and other imaginary buildings—all unbuilt and place-less. Though opulently described, these buildings are visited strictly through images and prose. Miniatures of imaginary buildings may aid the recall of literary experiences, but not of real places, and so are not souvenir buildings, they say.

Of course, many of architectural history's greatest buildings and most majestic monuments are, by now, mainly mythic and wholly insubstantial. Souvenir buildings represent many of this poignant, swelling, spectral population of buildings no longer among us. Prominent among these are world's fair buildings, often erected and taken down over the course of a couple of years. Their souvenirs may be the only remaining three-dimensional trace of these often extraordinary structures. That they are vanished does not prevent souvenir buildings provoking their recall. Still, the unbalanced enthusiasms of memory, over time, render these places, once real, increasingly fictive.

Another variety of architectural fiction is given form in a few, incautious souvenir buildings representing places not built as foreseen, or not built at all. For example, in 1925 preparations were made for a new St. Joseph's Oratory in Mon-

Three world's fair buildings, all demolished. (Left to right) Empire Exhibition, Glasgow, 1938; Wonderwall, New Orleans, 1984; Tower of Jewels, San Francisco, 1915

Below:
St. Joseph's Oratory, Montreal, as planned

treal. Plans were drawn and large well-detailed miniatures of "La Future Basilique" were cast to boost enthusiasm for the project, and, no doubt, assist with fund-raising. The building described by these prospective souvenirs is topped by a handsome hemispherical dome, raised up on a drum, and flanked by four, shorter, very slender towers resembling minarets.

It is often observed of plans that they change. St. Joseph's Oratory was completed in 1954. For reasons now obscure, but which may have to do with the

13

incomplete success of the fund-raising effort, the delicate dome depicted in the miniature was not built. Instead, the building is surmounted by an elongated scaleless lump, like the upturned, lopped-off end of a colossal football. Architectural historians will note the uncanny similarity between this dome and the dome of the Pro Football Hall of Fame in Canton, Ohio. Souvenirs have been cast of both buildings, and finished in gleaming copper. For Canadian acquaintances who have seen both "La Future Basilique" and the souvenir of the present St. Joseph's, the former represents a place simultaneously less real, and, paradoxically, more memorable.

St. Joseph's Oratory, Montreal, as built, with Pro Football Hall of Fame, Canton, Ohio

Very often, souvenir buildings arrive close on the heels of the places they portray, before enthusiasm for the new building wanes. This is especially true for the legion miniatures of commercial buildings cast to coincide with dedications and grand openings. These souvenirs, nearly always representing buildings only a banker, industrialist, real estate developer, or collector could love, were usually produced once, and never again.

Still, with some of the world's ancient monuments and other celebrity buildings, the production schedule for souvenir buildings is both looser and more enduring. Thousands of years passed between the completion of the pyramids and Sphinx at Giza and the first appearance of their mass-produced miniatures. Replication of the Eiffel Tower continues at a breakneck pace, more than a hundred years after the last girder was riveted in place.

Consider a miniature of the Colossus of Rhodes, which may or may not have straddled the harbor entrance at that Mediterranean seaport but in any event is counted among the ancient world's seven wonders. This brass casting was conceived long after the great monument either did, or did not, topple into the sea. Is this a souvenir building? If so, it is of a different order, stirring tourists' memories of speculating over a colossal absence at Rhodes.

While the definition of souvenir buildings is a little elusive, the *idea* of them appears, at first, wholly unlikely. The words *souvenir* and *building* are an unsuited pair, each everything the other is not.

Souvenirs are slight, inexpensive trifles. Buildings are substantial, enduring, and costly. Souvenirs must be small to be portable. Buildings may be enormous, and are rooted in their places. The ostensible purpose of many souvenirs is to restrain paper against a breeze; buildings harbor the astonishing range of human activity.

Colossus of Rhodes, 1970s

15

The improbability of souvenir buildings contributes to their appeal, to the fun of them. The fun of kitsch is similar. Kitsch is also unlikely, as well as sentimental, low art, and anti-profound. An acquaintance recently returned from Hawaii with a kitsch "shell-o-saurus," a small dinosaur with large eyes fashioned from seashells.

There are many people who consider souvenir buildings kitsch. Collectors and other zealots deny this charge. Kitsch, they point out, distorts the familiar, and relies on general comic effect. Souvenir buildings reproduce the familiar, just smaller, and provoke every person's memory in dramatically different ways. If souvenir buildings involve kitsch, they are also more than kitsch—kitsch and more.

All of us are familiar with the pleasures of miniatures, and our experience of them begins early on. Almost all toys are miniatures, including the entire range of animals, vehicles, tools, machines, buildings, even people. Like toys, souvenir buildings reverse the everyday order of things. People become monumental, while the planet's tallest skyscrapers rise barely to the tops of our shoes.

This reversal is accompanied by a giddiness, like that of peering down from the top of the Empire State Building into the crowd of suddenly miniature Manhattan monuments far below.

There is a related pleasure, again like a child's pleasure, in grasping the figure of a great building and turning it over in our hands. Certainly, there is a thrilling, if illusory, force in this. The entire variety of architectural experience of a place occurs almost in an instant. A miniature building encourages us to see and touch every feature—its plan and massing; each turret, dome, and spire; all facades, even the roof—nearly simultaneously. Souvenir buildings, in this way, provide jolts of architectural essence.

Among academics, there is discussion of the haptic experience of architecture. This has to do with the importance of our sense of touch in understanding and inhabiting places. Indeed, the most agreeable buildings pay close attention to the parts of them we handle (doors, windows, cabinets, railings); tread upon (floors, stairs); sit and lie upon (benches, hearths, and, again, floors); and rub up against (e.g., walls, door frames).

Miniatures offer a surrogate haptic experience of the forms of whole buildings. Is it too much to claim that we better understand and inhabit real buildings through their souvenirs?

Urbanists, planners, and other hardheaded types may object that there is more to comprehending architecture and cities. When it comes to the built environment, they are right. Miniature buildings play the most diminutive roles.

It should not be forgotten, though, that all buildings, and many cities, begin life as miniatures. The design of the grandest construction starts with the tiniest sketches. Small-scale drawings and, perhaps, models follow. Additional detailed drawings are employed as blueprints for construction. This helps account for the fact that buildings provide unusually good models for miniatures, and that they are the largest objects effectively modeled at small scale. Topographic models defy ready comparison to even the most distinctive landscapes. Miniature mountain ranges have never taken hold, and we know of no souvenir replicas of the Grand Canyon.

Here, troublemakers might interject the premise that buildings are something like souvenirs of their architects' drawings and models. In fact, souvenir buildings are benign *agents provocateurs*, working, like the buildings they represent, the widest range of our recollections. It is an irony that souvenir buildings nearly never cause us to think only of buildings. Instead, our memories of places, at particular moments, are summoned whole.

A miniature of the Empire State Building prods our recall of the skyscraper, certainly, and perhaps its history. With this, though, a visit to New York comes to mind, a visit enjoyable and/or painful, recently made or long ago, alone or accompanied by people still living or those now gone; in beautiful weather or foul; to places redolent of perfume/the East River/cooling madeleines; to see

Empire State
Building, 1930s

relatives/friends/business people;
Macy's/museums/the Mets; the Statue of Lib-
erty/Rockefeller Center/the Empire State
Building. This is the purpose of souvenir
buildings—to incite the profusion of memory.

This is also the marvel of souvenir buildings: that the identical miniature sparks in
each of us extravagantly different webs of
remembrance.

The recall of experience through
place seeks impressions, rather than any
searing urban truths. Souvenir Empire
State Buildings reveal mercifully little of
the Platonic form of New York City.

Buildings and
Souvenir Buildings

L AST YEAR, NEARLY FOURTEEN MILLION PEOPLE VISITED SAN FRANCISCO. According to the Visitors and Convention Bureau, the city's six most popular destinations are Fisherman's Wharf, Chinatown, the Golden Gate Bridge, Union Square, cable cars, and Golden Gate Park. Others have observed that the favorite building in Everyone's Favorite City is a bridge.

Although there are miniatures of only one of these places (yes, the bridge), San Francisco is well represented in the world of souvenir buildings. The Ace Architects collection includes replicas of three generations of the Cliff House, Coit Tower, the Ferry Building, Golden Gate Bridge, Mission Dolores, Tarantino's Restaurant, the Telephone Exchange Building, the Tower of Jewels, and the Transamerica Pyramid. Per capita, San Francisco's population of souvenir buildings exceeds that of New York.

The city's visitors are offered a wide range of tours. Among the more intriguing sounding are "Exotic Alleys and High Society," a tour of places described in mystery novels and suspense thrillers; "Brothels, Boarding Houses, and Bawds," focusing on past and present red light districts; and "Near Escape," a tour of haunted places, including the old cemeteries in Colma.

We propose an addition to this list, "Souvenir San Francisco," a tour of four buildings represented by souvenir miniatures.

First stop is Coit Tower, erected in 1933 as a tribute to the city's firemen.

Coit Tower, San Francisco

Souvenir Coit Tower, ca. 1930s

Wags point out the resemblance of this monument to an upturned fire hose nozzle. The Tower's souvenir, rising above six inches, also dates from the 1930s, and is massed and detailed with unusual fidelity. Both the Tower and its souvenir are cast, the former in concrete, the latter in lead.

The Golden Gate Bridge was completed in 1937, and has become the city's most familiar landmark. The span's earliest miniature, a circa 1940 copper-plated pot-metal casting, is imprinted "Souvenir of Golden Gate Bridge." The addition of this description was a wise decision, for the replica is so clumsily and apparently carelessly wrought that it might be mistaken for some other bridge. That this sorry

Golden Gate Bridge, San Francisco

Souvenir Golden Gate Bridge, ca. 1940

souvenir causes us to think of the elegant structure of the Golden Gate Bridge is evidence of the force of language and memory.

In fact, this souvenir is something of a fraud. A replica titled "George-Washington-Bridge-New York," was produced from a mold nearly identical to its West Coast twin. Because the New York casting is sharper, it is likely the earlier souvenir, perhaps dating from the years just following the George Washington Bridge's opening in 1931. While most miniature buildings take liberties with their subjects, the counterfeit souvenir of the Golden Gate Bridge is a candidate for the Hall of Chutzpah.

Souvenir George Washington Bridge, New York, ca. 1930s

Transamerica Pyramid, San Francisco's trademark, if still controversial high-rise, was completed in 1972. One of its several souvenir miniatures is well detailed in plastic, molded in 1985. This replica is faithful to the pyramid's massing and vertical proportions, while casting the windows as horizontal ribs, and, breathtakingly, adding an apparently twenty-story thermometer to the building's inclined facade. The intent of this last liberty is to render the souvenir useful, as though the provocation of human memory is too slight a purpose.

Overlooking Seal Rock and the Pacific Ocean, the often fog-shrouded Cliff House perches on a site that has been home to a succession of buildings, the first appearing in 1863. This burned in 1894, and was rebuilt as Victorian Folly, which burned in 1907. Portions of the now-standing Cliff House date to the rebuilding of 1908.

The Cliff House's several souvenir buildings offer something like stop-action photography of the place, only at very long intervals. The earliest miniature was cast in lead for the 1915 Panama Pacific Exposition in San Francisco, and models a repressed classical cube. The next souvenir, a copper-plated pot-metal casting produced in Los Angeles in the late 1940s, is a profusion of nondescript additions and signs. The most recent miniature, a circa 1960 Japanese pot-metal casting, pictures

Transamerica Pyramid, San Francisco

Souvenir Transamerica Pyramid, 1985

Cliff House, San Francisco

Souvenir Cliff House, 1915

Souvenir Cliff House, 1940s

Souvenir Cliff House, 1960s

a modern-styled street frontage, with only a trace of the original 1908 building still visible. Each of the landmark's three generations of miniatures has survived the structure it represents. The surprise is that the building is so changeable, while its souvenirs are so enduring.

If the difference between buildings and their miniatures is a commonplace, then the close relations between the two come as something unexpected. Whereas real buildings are large, fixed, singular, inhabitable, and reveal themselves gradually, their souvenirs are tiny, mobile, legion, and uninhabitable except through memory, and instantly available to our curiosity.

In each of its iterations over time, the Cliff House has been made and remade to meet an unusually transient set of purposes and enthusiasms. The place has passed, evidently, through many hands, and it is unlikely that anyone involved in the 1908 building of the Cliff House remains alive. Yet the life of their building continues, if along a line they had not foreseen.

In 1915, the late 1940s, and circa 1960, souvenir miniatures were made of the Cliff House. The shared purpose of these enterprises was to make money by serving the purposes of memory. It is doubtful that any of those who made the 1915 souvenir survive, the Los Angeles plant where the 1940s replica was cast has long ago closed, as has the Japanese foundry which produced the Cliff House's last miniatures. Still, the souvenir buildings carry forward, passed from those who originally purchased them, to others, and to others again, along an unpredictable path.

With each changing of hands over time, both the Cliff House and its miniatures are reimagined. Old memories are edited or entirely shed, while more present memories attach themselves until the next changing of hands. Both building and souvenir persist, though, ever outliving memory, while provoking it.

Architectural History and the History of Souvenir Buildings

I n 1896, two Banister Fletchers, father and son, first published *A History of Architecture on the Comparative Method*. The son, eventually dubbed Sir Banister, carried forward the book's periodic revision and udpating for the rest of his life.

Currently in the nineteenth printing, the late Sir Banister's standard runs to nearly seventeen hundred pages of single-spaced ten-point type and black-and-white illustrations, and includes discussion of thousands of buildings, while weighing in at a formidable six pounds. Describing this book as thorough, even comprehensive, underappreciates the scope of its ambition.

A History of Architecture (the title, though nothing else, has shortened over the years) includes *very* few buildings of which there are souvenir miniatures. The minuscule area of overlap takes in only the most familiar of architecture's ancient monuments (the Sphinx and pyramids, Parthenon, Pantheon); the best-known devotional structures (the Taj Mahal and a smattering of European Romanesque, Gothic, and Baroque churches and cathedrals); as well as a few of the usual modern suspects, especially New York and Chicago skyscrapers.

History employs a method for organizing the past. Sir Banister arranges *A History of Architecture* into seven chapters, founded on place and period. Buildings are grouped and discussed formally, and according to style. Altogether, the book aspires to elucidate the progress of architecture from prehistory through to the late twentieth century.

Is it surprising, then, that *A History of Architecture* overlooks Elvis's Graceland? Sir Banister's *History* also neglects Shakespeare's thatched cottage, Lincoln's log cabin, and Will Rogers's stone tower in Colorado. Omitted, for clarity, are the Jefferson Memorial and the Alamo; the capitol buildings of Illinois, Louisiana, Missouri, and Cuba; world's fairs in Brussels, Chicago, New York, San Francisco, and Scotland; the Egyptian Revival People's United States Bank in St. Louis, Corn Palace in Mitchell, South Dakota, and Pagoda in Reading, Pennsylvania. There are souvenir buildings of and from all these places.

Souvenir buildings, as a group, offer something like an alternative, shadow history of architecture. This history is popular, rather than academic. It is largely unconcerned with period, place, style, and the inexorability of progress; instead it focuses on the range of buildings people have thought remarkable, important, appealing, and worthy of a souvenir. Souvenir architectural history includes all those places made miniature, which spur memory.

In the United States, unlike the rest of the world, these buildings include the obscure, unusual, modest, and workaday, as well as the obligatory monuments. Among U.S. souvenir buildings are scores of suburban banks from the 1950s and 60s, as well as dozens of small-town banks from the teens, 1920s, and 30s; college administration buildings and football stadiums; factories, grain elevators, and silos; the Goodyear dirigible hangar in Akron, Ohio, and Hoover Dam on the Colorado River; the "Chapel in Holy City Near Craterville Park, Okla." and "Zembo Mosque, Harrisburg, Penn."; Whitman National Monument in Walla Walla, Washington; and a pair of architectural pachyderms—the Elephant Tower from the 1939 Golden Gate International Exposition in San Francisco and Lucy the Elephant, still standing in Margate, New Jersey.

In addition to their very moderate celebrity these places share two qualities crucial for subjects of souvenir buildings. All are/were easily accessible and on the beaten track, or not far from it. It is a shortsighted vendor who offers souvenirs of places impossible to visit. More importantly, all these places are/were memorable, and in affirming rather than discouraging ways. There are few souvenirs of entirely forgettable buildings and fewer still of dismal places.

Interestingly, three places associated with presidential assassinations are included among souvenir buildings. In addition to a replica of Dealey Plaza in Dallas, there are miniatures of Lincoln's Tomb in Springfield, Illinois, and the Garfield Memorial in Cleveland. If tragedy surrounds these places, the need to remember and obligation to mourn are at the hearts of their souvenirs. Consider the buildings not made as souvenir miniatures: prisons; crematoria and mausolea; supermarkets and shopping malls; fire and police stations; post offices and classrooms; gas stations; neither the FBI nor CIA headquarters, though a miniature Pentagon has been cast; the Vietnam Veterans Memorial, though there are souvenir replicas of the Lincoln and Washington Memorials, as well as the Holocaust Museum; every project designed by Michael Graves, Robert Venturi, Frank Gehry, as well as almost every building designed by Philip Johnson, save the Seagram Building and Lincoln Center.

Here, with the exception of work by the four famous architects, souvenir architectural history's roster of excluded buildings largely overlaps that of *A History of Architecture*. Would Sir Banister's shade be pleased with this common ground?

The unsympathetic and unsentimental may argue that souvenir buildings, rather than suggesting a shadow architectural history, record little more than the outcome of a popularity contest. If, in this contest, the prevailing buildings are those proven memorable, and the vanquished are drawn from the list of prisons, shopping malls, gas stations, and other forgettable places unworthy of a souvenir, then popularity appears one wholly reasonable measure of architecture. Souvenir buildings provide a trace, over time, of this measure, and of a body of architecture worth remembering.

If souvenir buildings shadow history, they, like the buildings they represent, also possess a history. Unlike architectural history, the history of souvenir buildings began a little more than one hundred years ago, with the rise of popular tourism in Europe and the celebration of the United States Centennial in 1876.

Of course, the phenomenon of miniature buildings stretches into prehistory, and forms part of many cultures' historic legacy. Museums contain tiny temples from classical Greece and Dynastic China and miniature monuments from ancient Egypt and Pre-Columbian America.

The earliest miniatures in the Ace collection include appealingly detailed bronze castings of the Temple of Hercules and Trajan's Column in Rome; the Colonnes de Juillet and D'Austerlitz as well as the Obelisk de Luxor in the Place de la Concorde in Paris; and Cleopatra's Needle, the Egypt-ian obelisk on the Thames Embankment, London. These souvenirs date from the third quarter of the nineteenth century.

Souvenir buildings produced for the Centennial include a variety of iron castings of Boston's Old South Church and Philadelphia's Independence Hall. Also from this period are molded glass miniatures of Independence Hall and the Centennial Exposition's Memorial Hall, again in Philadelphia.

The teens, twenties, and thirties were the heyday of souvenir buildings. Highly detailed miniatures, often cast in lead and

Temple of Hercules, Rome; inkwell, bronze, ca. 1870

plated in silver, copper, or brass, were produced in the widest range of European and American places. Among the most attractive groups of souvenirs in the collection are the extraordinary variety of European churches, cathedrals, town halls, houses, castles, even public houses cast in this period.

Old South Church, Boston; coin bank, iron, 1876

An equally pleasing subcollection, produced during the first third of this century, includes as subjects only American banks and financial institutions. These miniatures represent the most architecturally articulate small buildings, all turned out in the narrow range of dependable and trustworthy styles—classical, Neoclassical, Georgian, Italian, and English Renaissance. Predictably, there are few examples of bank buildings in less decorous garb—Spanish, Baroque, Gothic, and Art Deco. The collection includes no examples of banks from this period gotten up in Tudor, Mannerist, Modern, or any kind of French dress.

Beginning in the late 1930s, souvenir buildings were increasingly cast in pot metal, a cheap stew of ingredients that includes zinc, tin, aluminum, and various "mystery metals." Pot metal takes to molds indifferently, unlike more expensive bronze and toxic lead, with which proficient casters achieved remarkable detail. From this point, the die, it might be said, had been cast. Once casting with pot metal began in earnest, in the late 1940s, the need for detailed models evaporated. That buildings from this period also became far less detailed cannot be explained

Hofbrauhaus, Munich;
coin bank, lead, ca. 1920

German American Bank,
Minneapolis; coin bank,
lead, ca. 1920

Banker's Life Company,
Des Moines; coin bank,
pot metal, 1939

by their souvenirs, though. *A History of Architecture* provides a more likely account.

In the 1940s, there was widespread retrenchment in the scope and variety of souvenir buildings. While miniatures of the major monuments were still cast, lesser and eccentric subjects were neglected. By the 1950s most of the production of sou-

First National Bank, Amarillo, Texas; pot metal, 1940s

Right:
United Nations Headquarters, New York City; pot metal, 1960s, made in Japan

venir buildings had been taken to Japan, where high-quality pot-metal souvenirs, of a very limited number of buildings, were cast until the 1970s.

Still, the craft of souvenir buildings has achieved its nadir only in the 1990s. With widespread use of detail-less molds, and materials exquisitely unsuited to casting, including pewter, resin, and so-called composition, miniatures of the most distinctive places are rendered just this side of unrecognizable. Recent advances in pewter casting bring hope. Still, the collection includes no souvenir buildings formed of resin or composition.

Not enough is known of those who manufactured the many more appealing souvenir buildings. While some castings bear their maker's name, more are marked only with their country of origin. The authors of the majority of souvenir buildings are an anonymous group.

First National Bank,
Arlington, Texas; resin,
1980s

Still, some skilled and prolific American manufacturers often did mark their issue. Beginning in the teens, the A. C. Rehberger Company in Chicago cast many of the bank building miniatures just mentioned. With these, the company name is nearly always stamped under the base.

Also during this period and in Chicago, Eugene Sigle cast a set of wonderfully detailed souvenirs of the city's aquarium, planetarium, natural history museum, and Board of Trade. Each includes their maker's initials, cast in the base.

Other American casters who marked their souvenir buildings include Almar, American Art Works, Art Metal Works, Banthrico, Bradley and Hubbard, Dodge, Green Duck, J. B. Company, K and O Company, Kenton Hardware, Robbins Com-

450 Lexington Avenue, New York;
pewter, ca. 1990

Arc de Triomphe, Paris; pot metal,
ca. 1990

pany, Robert Stoll, and Staybright Novelty. Of these, only Banthrico and the Rehberger Company continue to cast miniature buildings.

It is said, never with any real evidence, that every cloud possesses a silver lining. Even in this dark time in the history of souvenir buildings, there are some bright spots. By employing carefully crafted molds, new alloys, and advanced casting techniques, Dupliform Casting in Massachusetts produces terrific miniature buildings in pewter, of all things. A high point is their replica of the nearly new 450 Lexington Avenue in New York.

The French caster, Polyne, has developed a method for injecting molten pot metal into highly detailed molds. Souvenir buildings cast in this fashion are *très beaux,* though subjects are limited, *naturellement*, to the Eiffel Tower, Arc de Triomphe, and Notre Dame. *Quel dommage*!

Overleaf, clockwise, from the left:

Philadelphia. The large replica of Independence Hall (center), an iron coin bank, was cast for the United States Centennial in 1876. More diminutive miniatures, shown in the foreground, were cast in the 1960s and 1970s.

Clocks. What time is this place? The celluloid Trylon and Perisphere (front) is a windup clock. The Perisphere, ringed by twelve hour markers, turns *very* slowly. Time is read against the Trylon, which also sports a thermometer.

Italy. In the country that gave birth to futurism, the models for most souvenir buildings date from the Renaissance. Miniatures include (center, left to right) the Roman-era arena in Verona, Rialto Bridge in Venice, and St. Mary's in Florence with Giotto's Tower.

Vernacular. Almost always escaping the attention of architectural historians, but not of souvenir building makers, are those buildings unconcerned with style that people assemble for themselves. Pictured here are thatch roofed houses from Japan and the Phillipines, tepees in Wyoming, cliff dwellings in New Mexico, and Lincoln's Kentucky Log Cabin.

St. Peter's Basilica. Construction of the greatest church in Christendom consumed two centuries and the lives of a half-dozen architects, including Michelangelo. Thousands of these 8-inch-tall, well-detailed miniatures have been cast at a small foundry in Florence since the 1950s.

Power Generation. Hoover Dam holds back the wild, onrushing Colorado, generating the electricity required to light homes and turn the wheels of industry in the Southwest.

Finance and Insurance. Since the teens, banks and insurance companies have offered souvenir miniatures of their often unremarkable buildings. Three souvenir skyscrapers pictured here (rear left to right) are typical: Colorado State Bank of Denver, First National Bank of Chicago, and Life of Georgia.

Exposition Universelle, Brussels, 1958. A miniature of the modern-styled United States Pavilion (center) is caught in a crowd of Atomiums, the fair's theme building.

SOUVENIR BUILDINGS AND

GREAT LITTLE CITIES

SOUVENIR BUILDINGS AT WORK

ABSOLUTELY FABULOUS LITTLE BUILDINGS

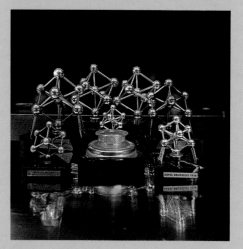

INDUSTRY AND METROPOLIS

Miniature Monuments

Little League of Nations

Souvenir Style

My Type of Place

It's a Small World's Fair

GREAT LITTLE CITIES

WHILE SOUVENIR BUILDINGS REPRESENT ARCANE, OUT-OF-THE-WAY PLACES, especially in the United States, more often they model urban structures. Cities provide, or should provide, an abundance of landmarks at once popular, accessible, and memorable—these qualities are shared by most monuments made in miniature form. Without them, places are less worth remembering and thus less worthy of being miniaturized.

Whereas one souvenir building can appear modest or out of place, when assembled with other little buildings it gathers force, provoking associations and recollections unexpectedly rich and complex. When miniature buildings of any great city are assembled, they achieve feats of urbanism surpassing the sum of their architectural parts.

The souvenir cities pictured here—collections of miniature buildings all hailing from the same place—aspire to no urban fidelities and liberties of all types are freely taken. Buildings are rendered with varying accuracy, at a variety of scales, and sited for pictorial effect. Sometimes, many representations of the same place are shown, such as souvenir Paris, which includes a baker's dozen Eiffel Towers. Still, our attention caroms from miniature to miniature, each time further provoked, and our cumulative memory is of the wide range of our own singular experiences of a great city.

Boston. A half dozen Bunker Hill monuments (front left) flank a miniature cityscape featuring City Hall, the Prudential Building, and Faneuil Hall. Beyond, at right, are a pair of Old South Churches, cast in 1876 for the Centennial.

London. A pair of Westminster Cathedral coin banks (center) frame a view toward the Masonic Peace Memorial and Temple Bar coin bank (beyond). Three Cleopatra's Needles loom in the background.

Paris. A miniature cityscape (front center) includes *tout de Paris*—the Eiffel Tower, L'Arc de Triomphe, Sacre Coeur, and Trocadero. The souvenir Centre Georges Pompidou (left front) was cast in Spain in the 1980s.

Rome. Souvenirs of the Eternal City include (left to right, center) the Pyramid of Caius Castius, Victor Emmanuel Monument, and Pantheon, all produced in the 1920s. Directly behind the monument is an especially well-detailed casting of St. Peter's, including Bernini's Arcade.

Washington, D.C. The city's monuments are framed by a miniature Capitol dome. The Capitol, topped by a red fez (right front), commemorates a 1928 gathering of Shriners. Souvenir Washington Monuments, cast in various sizes, line the horizon.

New York. Gotham's gang of high-rise souvenirs include several castings of the Flatiron Building (center), Woolworth and RCA buildings (right), as well as the former Pan Am Building (front right) fixed to a ruler and presented at the tower's opening in 1963.

Chicago. At the center of this Windy City rises the Wrigley Building, backed by the Prudential Building (left) and Sears Tower (right), and fronted by a well-detailed 19th-century lead casting of the Women's Christian Temperance Union.

San Francisco. Mark Twain complained that the coldest winter he ever spent was a summer in San Francisco. The city's fog-bound monuments, framed by the Golden Gate Bridge, include the Ferry Building (center) and Coit Tower (right). The Transamerica Pyramid rises behind Mission Dolores.

Los Angeles. Rising in the middle of this souvenir city of the angels is City Hall, a 1940s cast brass book-end. Castings of the Coliseum (left) were produced for the Olympic Games in 1932 and 1984.

SOUVENIR BUILDINGS AT WORK

WITH SOUVENIR BUILDINGS, FORM FOLLOWS FUNCTION INTO UNFAMILIAR territory. Imagine pencil sharpeners got up as the Chrysler Building, lamps in the form of St. Peter's in Rome, and just think what Frank Lloyd Wright would say about a lighter assuming the shape of his Johnson Wax Research Tower.

There is a compulsion for actual buildings to *do* something, to be useful and stay occupied. Idle and malingering buildings are met with unease and distrust. This extends to the world of souvenir buildings, where perfectly functionless miniatures are described as paperweights.

Mindful of these expectations, inventive souvenir makers have cast little buildings into a variety of useful objects, including salt and pepper shakers, cigarette and music boxes, ashtrays, clocks, coin banks, inkwells, thermometers, bookends, paper spindles, jewelry, bottles, bells, and candlesticks. Considering the foregoing, think of the necessary things not yet made as souvenir buildings—toasters and coffee makers, television sets, and washing machines. Imagine a refrigerator as the RCA Building, or a couch like the Roman Coliseum. Isn't it easy to see the glorious future of souvenir buildings in the next millennium?

The architect Bruce Goff remarked that, "In architecture, there's the reason you do something, and then there's the real reason." With souvenir buildings, despite the purposeless functions they entertainingly accommodate, their real reason remains the provocation of human memory.

Lamps. These illuminated buildings include three portable, glass and tin plate battery-powered lamps (right front) produced in Japan in the 1930s: (left to right) the Empire State Building, New York Aquarium, and Trylon and Perisphere.

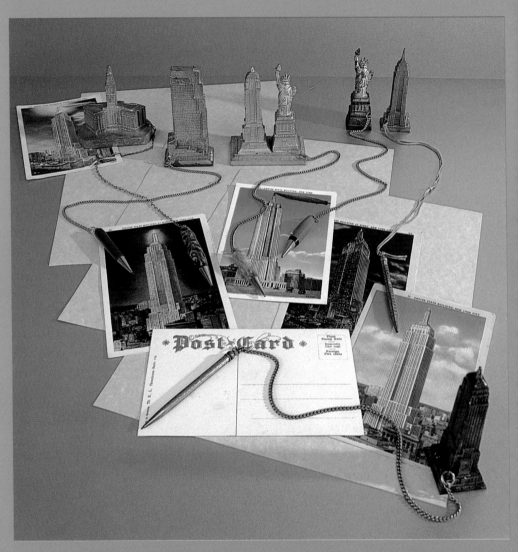

Pencil weights. To prevent pencils from getting lost, in the 1930s they were occasionally chained to buildings, including (left rear) Terminal Tower in Cleveland and the RCA Building in New York.

Thermometers. Obelisks and other vertical monuments make effective supports for thermometers. The makers of the miniature Sydney Opera House (front right), though, did not permit this convention to stand in their way.

Pencil sharpeners. Big pencils or little buildings? The most meticulously cast pencil sharpeners include figures of the Empire State and Chrysler buildings (center), produced in Germany in the 1930s. Replicas of St. Paul's Cathedral and Westminster Abbey in London (right center) were cast in 1956 as souvenirs of the Queen's coronation.

Sewing accessories. The Eiffel Tower pin cushion was assembled for the 1937 Exposition Universelle in Paris. The other souvenirs (left to right)—Pisa Tower, Cleopatra's Needle, and Temple Bar—are 19th-century English stamped brass needle cases.

Salt and pepper shakers. Like animals assembling for the Ark, most of these souvenirs come in pairs. While the earliest shakers here date from the 1930s, the majority were cast in Japan in the 1950s and 60s. The gear-shaped pair (front center) model the Ford Motor Company Rotunda at the 1933 Century of Progress World's Fair in Chicago.

European inkwells. While some souvenir building inkwells were cast through the 1940s, many more were produced in the 19th and early 20th centuries. The large, highly detailed brass double inkwell (center rear) represents an unknown, perhaps fictional, building. The pyramid inkwell was cast in Austria in the 1920s.

Cigarette lighters, ashtrays, and boxes. Anyone got a light? Souvenir building lighters, shown cocked, include (left to right) Big Ben, the Pan Am Building, Johnson Wax Research Tower, and Pisa Tower. The Yomeiomon Gate in Japan offers a horde of cigarettes, whereas, the Plaza de Toros in Madrid offers a place to stub them out.

Coin banks. To encourage thrift (and deposits), beginning in the teens, banks offered miniatures of their buildings with a slot for coins and, occasionally, a round hole for currency. Toronto's Traders Bank (center rear) is an especially fine, nickel-plated cast-iron bank, with separate slots for each family member.

Bookends. To hold a row of books, bookends have to be weighty and substantial. What then makes a better bookend than a building? Those pictured here are cast in iron and bronze, and include the Arco di Druso (left rear), Rome's Temple of Scipio (right rear), and Athens's Erechtheum (left front).

American desk pieces. The U.S. Fidelity and Guaranty Company souvenir (center), a brass-plated lead casting from the 1920s, is an inkwell and cigar box, whose lid includes a clock. The New York City skyline composite (left center) records the day and date.

LITTLE LEAGUE OF NATIONS

D URING MY TRIP WITH UNCLE CHUCK TWENTY YEARS AGO, I REMEMBER MAKING
some forgettable observation about German Gothic cathedrals. Uncle
Chuck responded, pointedly, that when these cathedrals were built, there was not
yet a Germany. So much for the idea of ancient architecture and national character.

Still, the miniature schlosses, rathauses, doms, munsters, and hofbrauhauses
forming most of Germany's population of souvenir buildings nearly always represent the medieval buildings favored by Romantics. The majority of French
souvenirs focus on châteaux and Gothic cathedrals. Constituents of Japanese
miniature buildings are almost all pagodas.

If a nation's souvenir buildings reflect little of its temperament, they are a measure of the sorts of places travelers have thought worth remembering. That the
types of places vary by country reveals both that differences remain in our increasingly undifferentiated world and that national distinctions remain drawn, at least in
some small part, architecturally.

Our memories of countries differ from our memories of cities. The largest
sprawling city seems coherent compared to the smallest country. The edges of
cities are often apparent, while the cartographer's lines are usually invisible. Too,
cities are tangible and relatively enduring, while countries appear abstract and,
lately, changeable. Rome is the Eternal City, yet we know of no Eternal Country.

Miniatures of the Pantheon, St. Peter's, and the Victor Emmanuel Monument
stir memories of a visit to this city. Souvenirs of the Palazzo Vecchio and St. Mark's
remind of Florence and Venice. Yet, do all these little buildings, taken together,
spur recollections of Italy? What miniature monument recalls its country the way a
little Coliseum recalls Rome? Like actual nations, our souvenir building–induced
memories are both less tangible and more abstract propositions.

France. Château du Chambord (front center) is backed by souvenirs of six cathedrals (left to right): Notre Dame de Bonsecours, Rheims, Chartres, Orleans, Strasbourg, and Notre Dame de Lorette.

Spain. Spanish souvenir architecture features Antoni Gaudí's Sagrada Familia and Casa Mila in Barcelona (center right), as well as the Christopher Columbus monument (rear center).

Egypt. The top of Giza's Great Pyramid (center) hinges open to provide a tomb for cigarettes. The pair of Sphinx bookends (rear) are iron castings, ca. 1930, while the pair flanking the pyramid were advertisements for a Mr. Spinks, a businessman, in St. Louis in the 1920s.

Germany. Except for the two smaller 1960s souvenirs (front), these highly detailed miniature buildings were produced in the teens and 1920s. They are all lead castings, plated in silver, copper, and brass.

Japan. One of the most affecting souvenir buildings is a miniature of the ruins of Hiroshima's domed Beaux Arts–style City Hall (center right).

England. Souvenirs of Blackpool Tower (left, front to back) include a 1930s brass match holder and striker; a 1920s silver-plated lead coin bank, cast in Germany; and an iron coin bank cast in England, ca. 1910.

Russia. Is it still called Red Square? Half a dozen little Russian monuments share the wall encircling the Kremlin. Among those made miniature are Lenin's Tomb (center right), a well-cast brass souvenir, served up on a green marble base.

SOUVENIR STYLE

SIR BANISTER FLETCHER'S *The History of Architecture* LEADS US, IN GREAT detail, through the Progress of the Styles. Architectural history is presented as a matter of succession—just as kings succeed kings, architects succeed architects, and styles succeed styles.

Yet history, everyone knows, repeats itself, perhaps more obviously in architecture than in other areas of human endeavor. Look at Classicism—in one guise or another, it has recurred in the Age of Pericles, Imperial Rome, the Renaissance, portions of the eighteenth century, portions of the nineteenth century, and throughout the twentieth century.

Recognizing that architectural styles never die, they just fade away and reappear, this section looks at six styles represented in the collection. Classical, no doubt, has come and gone more than any other style, though Gothic has had many revivals. Eclecticism may be said to characterize contemporary architecture, though some pundits view today's output as a rebirth of modernism. Islamic and vernacular influences adhere to buildings outside their own traditions.

Nations may rise and fall, but architectural styles endure. Each rebirth brings new twists, along with considerable similarity to prior incarnations. Souvenir buildings trace the rising and falling enthusiasms for styles. The plurality of styles contributes to enriching and democraticizing architecture. Through miniature buildings, we come to know these styles personally and are reminded that there are many ways to make a building.

Islamic. Many of these souvenir buildings, like their counterparts around the world, are intended to more than stir memories. Turkish mosques (center left and right) are lamps, while the miniature of the Mosque of Mansura in Algeria offers itself as, dare we say it, a paperweight.

Classical. The long arm of souvenir classicism begins with Athens's Erechtheum and Parthenon (left rear and center) and Rome's Temple of Hercules (rear center) to Berlin's Brandenburg Gate (foreground) and the Peace Arch (rear right) at the western border of Canada and the United States.

Gothic. Souvenirs of pointed architecture are the Palazzo Ca d'Oro (front right), draped in Venetian Gothic, the copper-plated Cologne Cathedral (center), and Rheims Cathedral (rear left).

American Eclectic. If many memorable United States souvenir buildings might be counted, by critics, among fashion's victims, they are slaves to no single style. In the front row (left to right) are a Renaissance themed section of the Wonderwall in New Orleans; the Classical Temple of the Jefferson Memorial; the Pagoda in Reading, Pennsylvania; and the Arabic-styled Corn Palace in Mitchell, South Dakota.

Modern. Deep thinkers continue to debate whether modernism is a style or something else. Still, a lot of these buildings look pretty similar, and make for surprisingly attractive souvenirs. Included here are the Air Force Academy Cadet Chapel (left front), Commercial National Bank of Ethiopia (left center), and the Edificio Italia (left top) in São Paulo, Brazil.

ABSOLUTELY FABULOUS
LITTLE BUILDINGS

I F, ON THEIR OWN, MOST SOUVENIR BUILDINGS APPEAR A LITTLE MODEST, LIKE MANY of the places they represent, they come off well in a crowd.

Still, some little buildings are real lookers, wonderfully made and detailed castings modeling especially satisfying architecture. This group includes a few of the most familiar monuments, among them St. Peter's in Rome, the Chrysler and Empire State buildings, and the Statue of Liberty in New York. But there are many miniatures of monuments with which we are less acquainted—the General Motors Building in Detroit, for example, the "Canopy Over Plymouth Rock," and the Kao Ye Shang Gen Ben Pagoda. There is a democracy in this; even an obscure building, if possessed of sufficient architectural talent, can make for a great miniature. Memory attaches to the range of places, well known and less so. Many buildings may be worth remembering, but only the fortunate will be summoned up with wonderful souvenir buildings.

Statue of Liberty. If Lady Liberty is not the scarcest souvenir, she is the most variable. The collection includes 100 examples, and no two are alike.

Empire State Building/Gotham Bank Building/Chrysler Building. This trio of New York's finest souvenir buildings are appealingly detailed lead castings from the 1920s and 30s.

New York Life Insurance Company, New York. Sibling castings of this Gotham skyscraper, the larger miniature was presented in the 1950s to agents selling a million dollars of insurance. The smaller casting was distributed at the building's opening in 1929.

Jarmulowsky Building, New York. This pair of cast iron souvenirs are similar, but not identical. The miniature at right reads "Presented by the Jewish Daily News," referring to an all-Yiddish newspaper published in Manhattan from ca. 1880 through the 1920s.

General Motors Building, Detroit. If there is a mother of all souvenir buildings, this miniature may be it. Cast in an era when it was claimed by the company's president that "What's good for GM is good for America," this well-detailed lead replica weighs in at a formidable three pounds.

Administration Building, Columbian Exposition, Chicago. This large cast-iron coin bank, retaining its original silver-and-gold finish, was first cast for the World's Fair in 1892 by the Kenton Hardware Manufacturing Company, which continued to produce this souvenir until 1913.

Canopy over Plymouth Rock, Massachusetts. This startlingly fine miniature is a silver-plated lead casting. The rock itself is barely visible within. This Baroque-styled monument was taken down in 1920, the 300th anniversary of the Pilgrim's arrival, and replaced with a nondescript classical pavilion.

Kao Ye Shang Gen Ben Pagoda, Japan. Text written in kanji, impressed into the base of this obscure souvenir, suggests that this miniature was cast to commemorate the 1,100th anniversary of the death of Master Hung Fa.

James A. Garfield Memorial, Cleveland. Every stone, window mullion, and roof tile is cast into this satis-fying souvenir of a little-known Romanesque-styled monument.

Rock Island Savings Bank, Illinois. Beginning in the early part of this century, banks distributed miniatures of their often impressive new buildings. This bank, turned out in full classical regalia, is an especially fine example, and dates from 1911.

Municipal Buildings and Campanile, Springfield, Massachusetts. The Massachusetts State Banker's Convention met in Springfield in 1912, and commemorated the get-together with this gold-flashed lead casting.

Industry and Metropolis

"Going down into the streets of a modern city must seem—to the newcomer at least—a little like Dante's descent into Hades," wrote Hugh Feriss in his 1929 work, *The Metropolis of Tomorrow*. Feriss, America's greatest architectural illustrator, proposed an antidote: "a species of tower buildings" that step back as they rise ever higher, permitting light and air to stream into the streets below. Feriss romanticized the then-new skyscrapers as man-made mountains, and, with mesmerizing drawings, made the case for tall, elegant buildings. This argument remains forceful and poignant.

Feriss draws the buildings of the future as handsome, often colossal. His drawings contrast both the past and present with the future, always to the latter's advantage, while revealing the pathos of the former. His perspective drawings of new, glorious, dramatically illuminated constructions are often framed by the darkened, wizened profiles of old houses, derelict factories, or out-of-date commercial buildings.

That what has come is less splendid than what Feriss foresaw is no reason not to remember his future, seen all the better with souvenir buildings.

Industrial Production. A darkened 19th-century factory frames the view of the new forms of industry (left to right): the Johnson Wax Research Tower, a high-rise grain elevator, and a soaring radio transmission tower.

View Toward Metropolis, 1930. This prospect, overlooking an imaginary gathering of skyscrapers, is framed by the rooflines and chimneys of rustic dwellings.

View Toward Metropolis, 1960. The darkened profiles of yesteryear's stepped towers frame the glowing crowded cubes of the new city.

New Tower. A souvenir of Chicago's Board of Trade Tower, cast from the clay of the building's excavations in 1929, stretches far above a street of classically attired banks.

New York. A monumental miniature of the Empire State Building dwarfs souvenirs of Union Dime Savings Bank (left) and 450 Lexington Avenue (right). The Woolworth, Chrysler, Empire State, and New York Life Insurance buildings rise in the background.

My Type of Place

During the Middle Ages, in the absence of books or common knowledge of writing, trade guilds arose in which the craft of one generation was passed on to the next. Most secretive of all the guilds were the masons, builders possessing the knowledge to make the great cathedrals stand up.

When focused on buildings rather than on kings and their architects, architectural history reveals an evolution of buildings by type—churches, houses, public works, and so forth. Each type has a history of its own, carried forward by designers who have developed specialized knowledge. Trade guilds in modern dress continue to operate today.

Souvenir buildings reflect our own modern, specialized skills, and thus may be grouped by type, ranging from dams to banks, from factories to monuments, and from stadiums to castles. Certain types lend themselves especially to particular nonmetal materials. Tall monuments make good-looking bottles, so they're often found in glass. Quantities of colorful promotional banks and ashtrays can be made inexpensively in ceramic.

The urge to cast a series of football stadiums as mementos of various alma maters is not difficult to comprehend. But who could predict the urge to cast a group of metal grain elevators? And why make so many different castings of Hoover (formerly Boulder, formerly Hoover) Dam—large, small, and smaller; fat and thin; squashed and elongated?

In the United States, especially, souvenir buildings of all types are created equal. Their quantity, stature, material, and quality have little to do with the usual hierarchies. The Ace collection is a souvenir democracy in which a factory is just as important as a cathedral (more so if it's a better casting), and a house may be bigger than Hoover Dam.

Stadiums. The figure of Knute Rockne towers over a miniature of Notre Dame Stadium (center). Engraved in the souvenir is his stirring rhyme. "For when the One Great Scorer comes to write against your name; He writes not that you won or lost, but how you played the game."

Holy Places. The souvenir Taj Mahal (center) is cast in brass and raised up on a white marble base. The miniature Oral Roberts Prayer Tower (center right) is in shiny gold plastic.

Monuments. Memorials to the war dead are erected in many countries. Several souvenirs pictured here are examples of this variety of monument. Included are memorials in Leipzig, Germany (middle center), Gettysburg (front center), and a melancholic soldier representing the World War I battle site in Ypres, Belgium (rear center).

Castles and Forts. The collection includes only one souvenir from the People's Democratic Republic of Yemen, the Lion Fortress (top center), set on wood grain plastic laminate.

Homes of the Famous and Obscure. The lid of the miniature of Shakespeare's House (rear center) opens to reveal a pair of inkwells. Fronting the Old Lady's Shoe is a copper-plated souvenir of "Death Valley Scotty's Original Castle" in California.

Factories and Grain Elevators. The souvenir of the French Worsted Company factory in Woonsocket, Rhode Island (front center), including a half dozen buildings and a pair of smokestacks, was cast in the 1920s.

Dams, Radio Towers, and Bridges. While the history of its name is murky, souvenirs describe themselves as "Boulder Dam," "Hoover Dam," and even "Hoover (Boulder) Dam."

Glass Souvenir Buildings. While most little buildings are cast in metal, the collection includes a variety of glass souvenirs. Fragile, transparent monuments include (front left to right) the Washington Monument, Flatiron Building, and Interstate Industrial Exhibition Building, cast for the 1873 Fair in Chicago.

Ceramic Souvenir Buildings. Another crowd of fragile, yet colorful, miniatures includes (top, left to right) the Bank of Delaware, First National Bank of Puerto Rico, an unidentified souvenir, and the Ohringer's Home Furniture Company.

IT'S A SMALL WORLD'S FAIR

ARCHITECTURE IS THOUGHT TO BE ENDURING. WHILE A FEW FAMOUS BUILDINGS have stood for millennia, almost all survive those who make and first inhabit them. The most anonymous, workaday structures often hold on for hundreds of years.

World's fair buildings, on the other hand, are ephemeral monuments, put up with the idea that they will soon be taken down. Free of the constraints and conventions that drag on other buildings, the landmarks of world's fairs are obliged, mainly, to be fun, stirring, and memorable. Is it any wonder that they have long provided wonderful models for souvenir buildings.

Paradoxically, world's fair miniatures are less ephemeral than the buildings they represent. The affecting Elephant and Sun Towers from the 1939 Golden Gate International Exposition are long gone, outlived by their souvenirs. The stirring Deco monuments of the 1933 Century of Progress World's Fair in Chicago, including the Hall of Science, Travel and Transportation and Federal Buildings, and Havoline Thermometer still endure, though only in miniature.

Several recent world's fair landmarks have escaped an early end. The Atomium in Brussels, Space Needle in Seattle, and Unisphere in New York are present in both life-size and in miniature form. Oddly, these modern monuments now seem tired, like a party gone on too long, while their souvenirs, and those of a dozen world's fairs before them, continue to excite our memories.

The World of Fairs. The phenomenon of world's fairs, begun in the late 19th century, proved difficult to sustain in the late 20th century. Pictured are fair buildings of all ages, including the Tower of Jewels (center), from the 1915 Panama Pacific Exposition in San Francisco; a pair of Space Needles (rear left), built for the 1962 fair in Seattle; and a monument from the 1936 Great Lakes Exposition in Cleveland (left center).

St. Louis World's Fair, 1904. Gold-flashed lead castings model the fair's Festival Hall (left rear and center), as well as the city's then newly completed Union Station (front right).

A Century of Progress, Chicago, 1933. A miniature of the fair's Sears Roebuck Building (center) is flanked by the Travel and Transportation Building (left) and the tri-towered Federal Building (right).

New York World's Fair, 1939. A dozen little Trylon and Perispheres frame a souvenir of the White Owl Cigar Exhibit (left center) and the fair's Administration Building (right).

Golden Gate International Exposition, San Francisco, 1939. Souvenirs of the Sun Tower encircle a painted plaster miniature of the fair's polychromed Elephant Tower.

COLLECTING SOUVENIR BUILDINGS

A FORAY INTO NEW ENGLAND, FERTILE TERRITORY FOR SEARCHING OUT SOUVENIR buildings, brought us to Concord, New Hampshire. Along Main Street is the handsome New Hampshire Savings Bank building, faced in the local stone, whose architectural style is of the 1930s. On first seeing this attractive building, we agreed it would make for an appealing miniature. We often say that of favored buildings. Driving past, we slowly realized that the miniature just proposed had been made, and that we had seen it, in fact, in our own collection. As Yogi Berra once observed, "it was like déjà vu all over again."

In the natural order of events, gathering souvenir buildings waits until our experience of a place is nearly complete and we have judged the experience worth remembering. For souvenir building collectors, this sequence of experience, judgment, and souvenir is often reversed, or altogether scrambled. The effect of this may be provocative, if sometimes a little disorienting.

With the Concord bank, for example, the building eventually caused us to recall our memory of its miniature. For us, then, the building became a souvenir of a souvenir building. The miniature Concord Savings Bank is well made and nicely detailed, cast in lead and silver plated. It was produced by American Art Works in Coshocton, Ohio, in the year following the bank's opening, and distributed to new depositors. This souvenir is also a coin bank, to encourage saving.

Long before seeing the bank in Concord, New Hampshire, we had found its miniature at a vast flea market in Long Beach, California. Before, the souvenir had always caused us to think of that market, of rising before dawn in order to arrive while vendors set up, walking the long rows in the brilliant sunshine, and first catching sight of the miniature bank. A most remarkable quality of miniature buildings is that they act as souvenirs, even though dissociated from the places they represent.

Concord Savings Bank, New Hampshire

The great majority of the two thousand–plus miniature buildings in our collection are souvenirs of places we may, or may not, ever visit. Miniature buildings representing places we hope to see are something like souvenirs of the future. Yet, a substantial set of recollections already adheres to every souvenir building. Each causes us to remember the circumstances of its discovery and addition to the collection (a market, shop, antique mall, even souvenir store; a letter or, better yet, a box; a tip, a trade, or a telephone call).

Increasingly, recent arrivals in the collection provoke thoughts of those who have generously urged them along our way. As we've sought out souvenir buildings, we've met or spoken with hundreds of others similarly possessed, and have enjoyed the pleasures of enthusing over our eccentric shared interests.

More surprising than the number of collectors are the diverse foci of their collections. We know of miniature building collectors interested exclusively in coin banks, or skyscrapers, or classical architecture, or places they have visited, or New York City, or Statues of Liberty, or small pieces, or large pieces, or pieces cast before 1940. The less restrained collect all souvenir buildings they find appealing. We have never met a cast-metal souvenir building we didn't like, and aspire to root them all out.

Also surprising is the range of people who collect souvenir buildings. Many are architects. Many more share only an agreeably soft spot for architecture. There are miniature building collectors who are doctors and dentists; contractors, real estate agents, and proprietors of auto repair shops; actors, "personalitites," writers, producers, directors, and set designers; students, unemployed, and retired; well-to-do, struggling, and somewhere in between; and children.

An article about our collection brought a letter from a boy who, with more than one hundred souvenir buildings, must be counted serious. He observed that although our collection is presently more extensive than his, he's only nine years old, and plans to be collecting for a long time.

Many miniature buildings make their way into the collection through the hands of these other collectors. There are trades, often small, though sometimes grand and elaborate, involving several collectors and souvenirs. There are purchases, usually modest, sometimes not. There are, as well, spectacularly generous gifts of the most desperately sought souvenir buildings.

The memories urged by these miniature places feature people, mostly, though other thoughts attach themselves. It is part of the appealing paradox of souvenir buildings that the recollections they summon are seldom only architectural.

835 Souvenir Buildings and Miniature Monuments

About the collection, there are three frequently asked questions: (1) What is your favorite souvenir building? (2) How many souvenir buildings do you have? (3) Who dusts?

We've narrowed the number of most favored miniatures, those we'd rescue from a burning building, to one hundred, indicated by a building. All these are carefully cast and finished, and are high examples of a not-high art. While many are scarce, our favorites also include the Empire State Building and Statue of Liberty. Less well known 1920s-era commercial buildings are well represented in our tiny pantheon, while 1960s-era skyscrapers are nearly absent. Exceptions include two really swell modern miniature monuments—the Commercial Bank of Ethiopia and the Edificio Italia in São Paulo, Brazil.

For collectors, we've indexed the relative scarcity of each souvenir building on the list. In instances where there exist a variety of souvenirs of a single building (for instance, we know of scores of different miniature Empire State buildings), this index applies to the easiest-to-find example. The Roman numeral I indicates the most common souvenir buildings, V the scarcest.

1. Aachen Dom, Germany III
2. Adler Planetarium, Chicago II
3. Administration Building, Colombian Exposition, Chicago III *
4. Aerial view of New York City V *

Aerial View of New York City; pot metal, ca. 1960, made in Japan

5. Alabama State Capitol, Montgomery, Ala. IV
6. Alamo, San Antonio I
7. Alaska Mutual Savings Bank, Anchorage II
8. Allegany State Park Lodge, N.Y. IV
9. Alliance Savings and Loan, Chicago II
10. Aloha Tower, Honolulu III
11. American Fletcher National Bank, Indianapolis II
12. American National Bank and Trust Co., Chattanooga, Tenn. III
13. Anacostia National Bank, Washington, D.C. III
14. Ann Hathaway's Cottage, Stratford-on-Avon, England II
15. Antonelliana Tower, Turin, Italy I
16. Antwerp Cathedral, Belgium III
17. Antwerp City Hall, Belgium IV
18. Anvers Cathedral, France IV
19. Arc de Triomphe, Paris I
20. Arch of Constantine, Rome III

21. Arco di Druso, Italy V
22. Arena di Verona, Italy III
23. Arlington Heights Federal Savings, Ill. III
24. Arsenal Savings and Loan Association, Indianapolis, III
25. Arsenal Tower, Kremlin, Moscow III
26. Aschenbecher Bruckler, Vienna IV
27. Assad Fortress, Peoples Democratic Republic of Yemen V
28. Astoria Memorial Column, Oreg. IV *
29. Atlantic City Lighthouse, N.J. V
30. Atlantic Savings and Loan V
31. Atomium, Brussels, Belgium II *
32. Aurora National Bank, Ill. III
33. Avenue State Bank, Oak Park, Ill. V
34. Bamburg Dom, Germany IV
35. Banco Coca, Ecuador IV
36. Bangor Savings Bank, Maine III *
37. Banker's Life Company, Des Moines, Iowa II
38. Banker's Trust, Ruan Center II
39. Banker's Trust Company, New York, N.Y. II
40. Bank of Delaware II
41. Bank of England, London III
42. Bank of Hawaii, Ltd., Honolulu IV
43. Bank of Korea IV
44. Bank of Madison, Wis. III
45. Bank of New Clarus, Wis. III
46. Barbara Fritchie's Home, Frederick, Md. IV
47. Baseball Hall of Fame, Cooperstown, N.Y. V
48. Basilica di Monte Berico, Vicenza, Italy IV
49. Basilica di Termoli, Termoli, Italy IV
50. Basilica San Marco, Venice II
51. Basilica S. Ligua di S. Antonio, Italy II
52. Basilica Vicenza, Italy V *
53. Basilique d'Albert, France V
54. Basilique de Notre Dame de Lorette, Arras, France IV

55. Bastille Monument, Paris III
56. Battle Monument, Bennington, Vt. III
57. Bayside National Bank of New York, N.Y. III
58. Beckley National Bank, W. Va. III
59. Beffroi de Lille, France III
60. Beringer Winery, St. Helena, Calif. II
61. Berlin Cathedral, Germany III
62. Berry Lincoln Store, New Salem, Ill. IV
63. Bethel College Administration Building, Tenn. III
64. Betsy Ross House, Philadelphia II
65. Beverly Savings, Chicago III
66. Big Ben, London IV
67. Birthplace of Robert Burns III
68. Blackpool Tower, England II *
69. Block House, Pittsburgh, Pa. IV
70. Board of Trade, Chicago II
71. Bolshoi Theatre, Moscow IV
72. B & O Queen City Station, Cumberland, Md. II
73. Borovitskaya Tower, Moscow IV
74. Boston Cityscape, Mass. V
75. Boulder Dam/Hoover Dam, Nev. II
76. Bowles Hall III
77. Brandenburg Tor, Berlin, Germany II
78. Breslau Rathaus, Germany IV
79. Brighton Pavilion, England IV
80. Broadmoor Hotel, Colorado Springs III
81. Brockton Hall, Mass. III
82. Bronx Hospital, Bronx, N.Y. III
83. Brookfield Federal Savings, Ill. II
84. Brooklyn Savings Bank in the Civic Center, N.Y. II
85. Bruges City Hall, Belgium III
86. Brussells Cathedral, Belgium III
87. Buckingham Palace, London III
88. Buena Vista Winery, Sonoma, Calif. III

89. Bunker Hill Monument, Boston II
90. Buon Consiglio, Trento, Italy IV

Cadet Chapel, U. S. Air Force Academy, Colorado Springs, Colorado; pot metal, ca. 1960, made in Japan

91. Cadet Chapel, U.S. Air Force Academy, Colorado Springs IV *
92. Calgary Tower, Canada I
93. Campanile, University of California, Berkeley III
94. Campanile, Venice II
95. Canada Monument, Ypres, France IV
96. Canon Mt. Aerial Tramway, Franconia Notch, N.H. III
97. Canopy over Plymouth Rock, Mass. V *
98. Cape Diamond Light III
99. Capitolio, Havana, Cuba V *

Capitolio, Havana; lead, 1930s

113

100. Capitol Records, Los Angeles IV
101. Capitol Savings, Olympia, Wash. III
102. Carcassonne, La Cité, France II
103. Carcassonne, Les Ramparts, France II
104. Carillon Tower, Stanley Park, Westfield, Mass. III
105. Carmel Mission, Calif. IV
106. Casa Loma, Toronto, Canada IV
107. Casa Mila, Barcelona III
108. Casino, Catalina Island, Calif. III
109. Casper National Bank, Casper, Wyo. V
110. Castello di Sirmione, Italy IV
111. Castello Normanno, Italy III
112. Castello Svevo, Termoli, Italy IV
113. Castillo de San Marcos, St. Augustine, Fla. I
114. Catalina Island, Calif. IV
115. Catholic Life Insurance, San Antonio, Tex. III
116. Centinela Valley Community Hospital, Inglewood, Calif. III
117. Central Bank of Tampa, Fla. III
118. Central National Bank and Trust, St. Petersburg, Fla. V
119. Centre Georges Pompidou, Paris IV
120. Century of Progress Buildings, Chicago, Ill. IV
121. Chalmers & Borton Grain Elevators, Hutchinson, Kans. IV
122. Chapel in Holy City, near Craterville Park, Okla. IV
123. Chapel Mite Bank, Chicago IV
124. Chartes Cathedral, France III
125. Chateau de Chambord, France IV
126. Chateau des Comtes, Ghent, Belgium V
127. Chateau Elan Winery, Braselton, Ga. III
128. Chelsea Savings Bank II
129. Chemeung Canal Trust Company, N.Y. II
130. Chesterton Rural Loan and Savings Association U.S. III
131. Chicago Federal Savings, Ill. II
132. Chittenden Trust Company, Burlington, Vt III
133. Christian Brothers Winery, St. Helena, Calif. I
134. Christian Science Building, New York World's Fair, N.Y. II
135. Christopher Columbus Monument, Barcelona II
136. Chrysler Building, New York, N.Y. I *
137. Church of the Archangel Michael, Moscow III
138. Church of the Assumption, Kondopoga, Russia III
139. Church of the Sleeping Mother of God, Kizhi Island, Russia III
140. Church of Transfiguration and Intercession & Bell Tower, Moscow III
141. Churchill Downs, Louisville, Ky. IV
142. Citizens Bank, Park Ridge, Ill. II
143. Citizens Bank and Trust Co., Tampa, Fla. V
144. Citizens Federal Centre, Dayton, Ohio II
145. Citizens Federal Savings, Cleveland, Ohio III
146. Citizens Federal Savings and Loan Association, Hammond, Ind. III
147. Citizens National Bank, Abilene, Tex. II
148. Citizens National Bank, Freeport, N.Y. V
149. Citizens Savings and Loan Company, Painesville, Ohio III
150. Citrus Tower, Clermont, Fla. IV
151. City National Bank, Tuscaloosa, Ala. V
152. City National Bank of Houston, Tex. III
153. City of Hope National Medical Center, Duarte, Calif. I
154. Clearing Bank, Chicago II
155. Cleopatra's Needle, London III
156. Cliff Dwellings, Bandolier National Monument, N. Mex. IV
157. Cliff House, San Francisco III
158. Cliff House, 1915, San Francisco IV *

159. Cliff House and Seal Rock, San Francisco IV
160. Clyde Savings, North Riverside, Ill. I
161. CN Tower, Toronto, Canada I
162. Coast Federal Savings & Loan Association, Los Angeles III
163. Coit Tower, San Francisco II *
164. College of Industrial Arts, Denton, Tex. IV
165. Collier Shot Tower Company, St. Louis, Mo. V *
166. Cologne Cathedral, Germany I
167. Colonne d'Austerlitz, Place Vendôme, Paris III
168. Colonne Julliet, Paris III
169. Colorado Federal Savings, Denver III
170. Colorado State Bank of Denver II
171. Colosseum, Rome II
172. Colossus of Rhodes IV
173. Coltejer, Medellin, Colombia V
174. Combined Insurance Building, Chicago III
175. Commerce Square, U.S. II
176. Commercial Bank of Ethiopia, Addis Abbaba IV *

Commercial National Bank, Shreve-port, Louisiana; inkwell, lead, 1930s

177. Commercial National Bank, Shreveport, La. V *
178. Commonwealth National Bank of San Francisco III
179. Compton Community Savings, Compton, Calif. IV
180. Conner Prairie Settlement, Ind. II
181. Continental Assurance Company, Chicago II
182. Continental Bank, Chicago III
183. Continental Products Inc., Chicago III
184. Cook County Federal Savings, Chicago II
185. Cooper River Federal Savings, U.S. IV
186. Corn Palace, Mitchell, S. Dak. II
187. Courthouse, Angelica, N.Y. IV
188. Coventry Cathedral, England IV
189. Cragin State Bank, Chicago V
190. Crestmont Savings, Maplewood, N.J. III
191. Culbertson Winery, Temecula, Calif. I
192. Dade Federal Savings, Miami III
193. Dahlstrom Administration Building, Jamestown, N.Y. IV
194. Dallas Cityscape, Tex. I
195. Danube Tower, Vienna IV
196. Darwen Tower IV
197. Dealey Plaza, Dallas, Tex. IV
198. DeLand Federal Savings, Fla. III
199. Den Danske Landmansbank, Denmark III
200. Des Moines Savings and Loan Association, Iowa III
201. Detroit Plaza, Mich. I
202. Devon Trust and Savings Bank, Chicago V
203. Die Wies Kirche, Steinhausen, Germany IV
204. D. L. Shackleford Motor Company IV
205. Dodger Stadium, Los Angeles II
206. Dollar Savings Bank, Pittsburgh, Pa. II
207. Dover Cooperative, Del. III
208. Drachenfels, Germany III

209. Durham Life Insurance Company, N.C. III
210. Dutch Wonderland, Lancaster, Pa. III
211. East Alton Savings and Loan, Ill. III
212. Easton National Bank, Pa. III
213. Equator Monument, near San Antonio, Tex. III
214. Edificio Italia, São Paulo, Brazil III *
215. Eglise Sainte-Gudule, Brussels, Belgium III
216. Eiffel Tower, Paris I
217. Einsiedeln, Germany IV
218. Eisenhower Chapel, Abilene, Kans. IV
219. Elephant Tower, Golden Gate Exposition, San Francisco V *
220. Emmanuel Evangelical Lutheran Church, Chicago V
221. Empire Exhibition Tower, Glasgow, Scotland V
222. Empire State Building, New York, N.Y. I *
223. Englewood State Bank, Englewood, Colo. III
224. Equitable Building, Chicago III
225. Erechtheum, Athens, Greece III
226. Erie County Savings Bank, Buffalo, N.Y. II
227. Eternal Light Peace Memorial, Gettysburg, Pa. III
228. Exchange Bank of St. Augustine, Fla. IV *
229. Exchange National Bank, Colorado Springs II
230. Expo Center, Vancouver, British Columbia, Canada II
231. Fall River Trust Company, Mass. III
232. Farmers and Mechanics Savings Bank, Framingham, Mass. III
233. Farmers and Merchants Bank, Lodi, Calif. IV
234. Faro di Piave, Piave, Italy III
235. Fayette National Bank and Trust, Ill. III
236. Federal Building, Century of Progress, Chicago IV *
237. Fernsehturm, Stuttgart, Germany V
238. Ferry Building, San Francisco III *

239. Festival Hall and Cascades, St. Louis Exposition, Mo. III *
240. Fidelity Federal Saving, Greenville, S.C. III
241. Fidelity Trust Company, Portland, Maine III *
242. Field Museum of Natural History, Chicago IV
243. First & Merchants National Bank (Pentagon), Washington, D.C. III
244. First Bank and Trust Company, Utica, N.Y. II
245. First Church of Christ Scientist, Boston II
246. First Federal Savings, Alhambra, Calif. III
247. First Federal Savings, La Porte, Ind. III
248. Federal Savings, Raleigh, N.C. III
249. Federal Savings and Loan, U.S. II
250. Federal Savings and Loan Assoc., Detroit III
251. Federal Savings and Loan Assoc., Elgin, Ill. II
252. Federal Savings and Loan Assoc., Greenville, S.C. II
253. Federal Savings and Loan Assoc., New Castle, Pa. III
254. Federal Savings and Loan Assoc. of Puerto Rico III
255. First Federal Savings of Berwyn, Ill. II
256. First National Bank, Amarillo, Tex. III

First National Bank, Davenport, Iowa; coin bank, lead, ca. 1930

257. First National Bank, Atlanta III
258. First National Bank, Casper, Wyo. IV
259. First National Bank, Davenport, Iowa V *
260. First National Bank, Denver, Colo. III
261. First National Bank, Des Plaines, Ill. II
262. First National Bank, Jackson, Mich. III
263. First National Bank, Montevideo, Minn. III
264. First National Bank, Neillsville, Wis. V
265. First National Bank, Riverside, Ill. II
266. First National Bank, Springfield, Ill. III
267. First National Bank, Sterling, Ill. III
268. First National Bank, Wamego, Kans. III
269. First National Bank, Warren, R.I. III
270. First National Bank, Woodbury, N.J. V
271. First National Bank and Central Wisconsin Trust Co., Wis. IV
272. First National Bank and Trust Co., Tulsa, Okla. III
273. First National Bank and Trust Co. of Floral Park, N.Y. IV
274. First National Bank of Glens Falls, N.Y. IV
275. First New Haven National Bank, Conn. III
276. First Security Bank, Salt Lake City, Utah III
277. First Security Trust and Savings Bank, U.S. III
278. First State Bank, U.S. III
279. First Wisconsin Bank, U.S. III
280. Flatiron Building, New York, N.Y. II *
281. Fletcher American National Bank, Indianapolis III
282. Fluor Building, Irvine, Calif. III
283. Forbes National Bank, Pittsburgh, Pa. III
284. Ford City Bank, Chicago III
285. Ford Motor Company, Belgium IV
286. Ford Rotunda, Century of Progress, Chicago III *
287. Fort Atkinson Savings and Loan, Wis. III
288. Fort Dearborn, Chicago II

289. Fort Snelling, Minneapolis I
290. Fort Wayne National Bank, Ind. II
291. Forty Fort State Bank, Pa. III
292. Forum, Rome II
293. Fountaingrove Round Barn, Santa Rosa, Calif. IV
294. Fountainhead Chiropractic Hospital, Davenport, Iowa III
295. 450 Lexington Avenue, New York, N.Y. IV
296. Frankfurt Rathaus, Germany IV
297. Franklin Trust Company, Paterson, N.J. IV
298. Frauenkirche, Munich, Germany III
299. Freedom Center, Chicago Tribune, Ill. III
300. Freiburg Munster, Germany IV
301. French Worsted Company, Woonsocket, R.I. IV *
302. Fullerton State Bank, Chicago V
303. Funkturm, Berlin, Germany III
304. Garfield Memorial, Cleveland, Ohio V *
305. Garmisch Partenkirchen Chalet, Germany III
306. Gate City Savings, Fargo Savings Center, N. Da. III
307. Gateway Arch, St. Louis, Mo. I
308. General Motors Building, Detroit II *
309. Genoa Lighthouse, Italy II
310. George Washington Bridge, New York, N.Y. III
311. George Washington Masonic Memorial, Alexandria, Va. II
312. Georgia State Capitol, Atlanta IV
313. German American Bank, Minneapolis IV *
314. Gettysburg Monument, Pa. III
315. Gettysburg National Bank, Pa. IV
316. Giotto's Tower, Florence II
317. Gnaden-Kapelle, Alt-otting, Germany V
318. Gold Dome, Buffalo, N.Y. III
319. Golden Gate Bridge, San Francisco I

320. Goodyear Zeppelin Airship Dock, Akron, Ohio III *
321. Gotham Bank, New York, N.Y. V *
322. Graceland, Memphis, Tenn. II
323. Grand Ole Opry House, Nashville, Tenn. IV
324. Gray Tower, Irish Hills, Mich. IV
325. Graz Clock Tower, Vienna, Austria IV
326. Great Lakes Exposition, Cleveland, Ohio V
327. Great Mosque of Mansura, Tlemcen, Algeria V
328. Great Northern Building and Loan, Chicago II
329. Great Wall of China, China I
330. Greenwich Savings Bank, N.Y. III

**Hall of Science,
Century of Progress,
Chicago; pen stand,
wood compostition,
1933**

331. Hall of Science Tower, Century of Progress, Chicago V *
332. Hamburger Rathaus, Germany III
333. Harlem State Savings Bank, Staten Island, N.Y. V
334. Harleysville National Bank and Trust, Pa. III
335. Harris County Domed Stadium, Houston, Tex. II
336. Harvard Stadium, Cambridge, Mass. III

337. Harvey's Resort Hotel, Stateline, Nev. II
338. Hattiesburg Savings and Loan, Miss. IV
339. Haus Wachenfeld, Bavaria, Germany IV
340. Havoline Tower, Century of Progress, Chicago I
341. Heidelberg Schloss, Germany III
342. Heights State Bank, U.S. III
343. Heritage County Bank II
344. Hermitage, Nashville, Tenn. IV
345. Hill 60 Monument, Ypres, Belgium IV
346. Hiroshima City Hall ruins, Japan IV
347. Hofbrauhaus, Munich, Germany V *
348. Hohenzollern, Germany IV
349. Holocaust Museum, Washington, D.C. II
350. Holstentor zu Lubeck, Germany III
351. Home Federal Savings, Chicago, Ill. II
352. Hong Kong Savings Bank III
353. Hoosac Mountain Tunnel, Mass. II
354. Hoover Limited Factory, London IV
355. Hotel New Otani IV
356. Hot Springs Mountain Tower, Ark. III
357. Houses of Parliament, London IV
358. Illinois Memorial Stadium, Urbana/ Champaign, Ill. IV *
359. Illinois State Capitol, Chicago IV *

**Independence Auditorium,
Missouri; bookends, iron, 1920s**

360. Improvement Federal Savings and Loan, Aurora, Ill. II
361. Independence Auditorium, Mo. IV *
362. Independence Hall, Philadelphia II
363. Inland Trust and Savings Bank, Chicago IV *

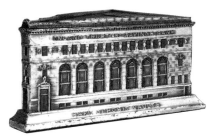

Inland Trust and Savings Bank, Chicago; coin bank, lead, 1920s

364. International Building, Credit Union Center, Madison, Wis. III
365. International House, University of California, Berkeley IV
366. Interstate Industrial Exposition, Chicago IV *
367. Iolani Palace, Honolulu II
368. Iowa-Des Moines National Bank, Iowa III
369. I Quatro Mori, Livorno, Italy III
370. Ivan's Bell Tower, Moscow II
371. Iwo Jima Monument, Washington, D.C. II
372. James Gamble Nippert Stadium, University of Cincinnati, Ohio V
373. Jarmulowsky Building, New York, N.Y. IV *
374. Jefferson Memorial, Washington, D.C. II
375. Jefferson Standard Life Insurance Company, Greensboro, N.C. III
376. Jerusalem Cityscape, Israel III
377. John Brown's Fort, Harper's Ferry, W. Va. IV
378. John Hancock Center, Chicago III

379. John Hancock Life Insurance Co. (Addition), Boston III
380. John Hancock Tower, Boston III
381. John Howard Payne's Home, Easthampton, N.Y. IV
382. Johnson Wax Research Tower, Racine, Wis. III *
383. Joliet Federal Savings, Ill. III
384. Keene National Bank, N.H. III
385. Key Biscayne Savings & Loan, Fla. III
386. Kimball Trust & Savings Bank, Chicago IV
387. Kings Dominion Tower, Richmond, Va. II
388. Kings Island Tower, Columbus, Ohio II
389. Kinkakuji Temple, Kyoto, Japan II
390. Kissing Bridge, U.S. III
391. Knights of Columbus, New Haven, Conn. III
392. Kraft International Headquarters, Chicago II
393. Kraybill Mennonite School, Mount Joy, Pa. IV
394. Kremlin Water Tower, Moscow III
395. Kress Building, Houston, Tex. V
396. La Cathedrale Luxembourg IV
397. La Giralda, Seville, Spain II
398. La Grotte de Lourdes, France II
399. Lamar Life, Jackson, Miss. III
400. Lansing Savings and Loan Association, Mich. III
401. La Nuestra Señora de la Reina de Los Angeles IV
402. La Porte Chaussee, Verdun, France V
403. Lawn Savings, Evergreenpark, Ill. II
404. Leaning Tower, Pisa, Italy II
405. Lefcourt State Building, New York, N.Y. IV
406. L'Eglise Bonsecour, France IV
407. Le Havre lighthouse, France III
408. Leipzig City Hall, Poland IV
409. Le Mont St. Michel, France II
410. Lenin's Tomb, Moscow III

411. Le Sacre Coeur, Paris II
412. Le Trocadero, Paris IV *
413. Life and Casualty Company of Chicago IV
414. Life of Georgia, Atlanta III
415. Lincoln Center/Empire State Building/Statue of Liberty, New York III
416. Lincoln Memorial, Washington, D.C. II *
417. Lincoln's Birthplace, Ky. II
418. Lincoln's Home, Springfield, Ill. II
419. Lincoln's Tomb, Springfield, Ill. II
420. Liseux Cathedral, France III *
421. Litchfield Cathedral, England III
422. Little America, Wyo. III
423. Little Brown Church, Nashua, Iowa II
424. Live Stock National Bank, Chicago III
425. Logan Square State & Savings Bank, Chicago V
426. Loggia fra Giocondo, Verona, Italy IV
427. Los Angeles City Hall, Calif. IV *
428. Los Angeles Memorial Coliseum, Calif. III
429. Louisiana State Capitol, Baton Rouge, La. III *
430. Lucy the Elephant, Margate, N.J. II
431. Lynchburg National Bank and Trust Co., Va. IV
432. Mackinac Island Blockhouse, Mich. III
433. Madison Square Garden, New York, N.Y. IV *
434. Madonnina dell'Angelo, Caorle, Italy IV
435. Mainz Dom, Germany IV
436. Maison du Roi, Brussells V
437. Malgesine, Italy IV
438. Malines Cathedral, Belgium III
439. Manhattan College, Riverdale, N.Y. IV
440. Marconi Savings and Loan Association, U.S. IV
441. Maria Zell, Vienna, Austria IV
442. Marina City Towers, Chicago IV
443. Mark Twain's Home, Hannibal, Mo. III

Madison Square Garden, New York; pot metal, 1980s

Masonic Temple, Chicago; box, lead, ca. 1920

444. Martin Nash Mortor Co., Atlanta V
445. Martintoren, Groningen, Holland IV
446. Maryland Casualty Company, Baltimore IV *
447. Masonic Temple, Chicago IV *
448. Mathias Monument, Budapest, Hungary IV
449. McKinney Stable, Cuba, N.Y. IV
450. McPherson County Courthouse, Kans. II
451. Melrose Park State Bank, Ill. V

452. Memorial Hall, Centennial Exposition, Philadelphia V *
453. Mennonite Church, Pa. III
454. Merchants Bank, Allentown, Pa. III
455. Merchants National Bank and Trust Co., Indianapolis III
456. Metropolitan Life Insurance Company, New York, N.Y. III *
457. Metz Cathedral, France III
458. MGM Grand Hotel, Las Vegas, Nev. I
459. Miami Beach Federal Savings (later), Fla. II
460. Miami Beach Federal Savings and Loan Assn. (earlier), Fla. III
461. Michaelskirche, Hamburg, Germany III
462. Mid Kansas Federal Savings, Kans. III
463. Midlands Maltings, Birmingham, England IV
464. Mid-West National Insurance Companies, U.S. II
465. Milan Cathedral, Italy II *
466. Minneapolis Milling Co., Minneapolis IV
467. Miramare, Trieste, Italy IV
468. Mission Dolores, San Francisco IV *
469. Mission San Gabriel, Calif. III
470. Mission Ventura, Calif. III
471. Missouri State Capitol, Jefferson City, Mo. III
472. Modern Woodmen of America, Rock Island, Ill. IV
473. Montgomery Ward, Baltimore IV
474. Monticello, Va. IV
475. Monument Manneken Pis, Brussels, Belgium II
476. Moreschi Building, Washington, D.C. III
477. Mormon Tabernacle, Salt Lake City, Utah I
478. Mormon Temple, Salt Lake City, Utah I
479. Mountain Springs Hotel, Ephrata, Pa. III
480. Mt. Greylock War Memorial, Lanesborough, Mass. II
481. Mt. Rushmore, Keystone, S. Da. II

482. Munich Radio Tower, Germany III
483. Munich Rathaus, Germany III
484. Municipal buildings and campanile, Springfield, Mass. IV *
485. Murache Castle, Sardinia IV
486. Museum of Science and Industry, Chicago IV
487. Natick Federal Savings Building, Mass. III
488. National Bank of Albany Park, N.Y. III
489. National Bank of America, Chicago V
490. National Bank of America, Paterson, N.J. V
491. National Bank of Commerce, Jackson, Tenn. III
492. National Bank of Commerce, Kansas City, Mo. IV *
493. National Bank of Cortland, N.Y. IV
494. National Bank of Norwalk, Conn. III
495. National City Bank of Evansville, Ind. V
496. National Label Company, Philadelphia IV
497. National Shrine of the Immaculate Conception, Washington, D.C. I
498. National Tower, Gettysburg, Pa. IV
499. NCR Auditorium, U.S. III
500. NCR Schoolhouse, U.S. III
501. Nebraska State Capitol, Lincoln, Nebr. IV
502. Neil House, Columbus, Ohio III
503. Neuschwanstein, Germany III
504. New Army and Navy Hospital, Hot Springs, Ark. IV
505. New Britain Federal Savings & Loan Association, Conn. III
506. New First National Bank, U.S. IV
507. New Hampshire Savings Bank, Concord, N.H. III
508. New Method Book Bindery Incorporated, U.S. III
509. Newport Balboa Savings and Loan Association, Calif. III

510. New York, N.Y. II
511. New York Aquarium, New York, N.Y. IV
512. New York Cityscape II
513. Nicolskoya Tower, Kremlin, Moscow III
514. Noel State Bank, Chicago IV
515. Northern Life Tower, Seattle, Wash. II
516. Northern Trust Company, Chicago II
517. Northwestern Electric Equipment Company, St. Paul, Minn. V
518. Northwest Federal, U.S. III
519. Norwood Savings and Loan Association, Chicago III
520. Notre Dame, Paris II
521. Notre Dame de Bonsecours, France IV
522. Notre Dame de Fourviere, France IV
523. Notre Dame de la Garde, Marseilles, France IV
524. Notre Dame de Lorette, France IV
525. Notre Dame de Lourdes, France II
526. Notre Dame Stadium, South Bend, Ind. III
527. Nurnburg, Germany III
528. Nutley Savings, N.J. III
529. Oak Lawn Federal Savings, Ill. II
530. Oakwyn State Bank, Berwyn, Ill. V
531. Obelisk, Place de la Concorde, Paris III
532. Occidental Center, Los Angeles III
533. Octagon House, Friendship, N.Y. IV
534. Octogon zu Wilhelmshohe, Germany V *
535. Ohio State Stadium, Columbus, Ohio II
536. Ohringer Home Furniture Co., Braddock, Pa. III
537. Old Capitol Bank & Trust Company, Corydon, Ind. III
538. Old Colony Church, Bishop Hill, Ill. III
539. Old Lady's Shoe II
540. Old Luthern Church, Trappe, Pa. IV
541. Old Main, Pennsylvania State College, Pa. IV
542. Old Matt's Cabin, Ark. II
543. Old Mill, Milledgeville, Ill. III
544. Old School House, Valley Forge, Pa. IV
545. Old Second National Bank, Aurora, Ill. II
546. Old South Church, Boston IV
547. Old Taylor Distillery, Frankfort, Ky. II
548. Olympic Savings, Berwyn, Ill. II
549. One Wacker Drive, Chicago V *
550. Oral Roberts University Tower, Tulsa, Okla. III
551. Ordway Building, Oakland, Calif. IV
552. Original Tower, Irish Hills, Mich. IV
553. Orlando Federal Savings, Fla. III
554. Orleans Cathedral, France III
555. Oslo Church, Norway IV
556. Pacific Mutual Life, Los Angeles IV *
557. Pacific Nations Exposition, Vancouver, B.C. V
558. Pagoda, Reading, Pa. III
559. Pahaska Teepee, Yellowstone, Wyo. IV
560. Palais d'Angkor Wat, Thailand IV *
561. Palais de Chailot, Paris IV
562. Palazzo Ca d'Oro, Venice IV
563. Palazzo Ducale, Venice IV
564. Palazzo Vecchio, Florence II
565. Palazzo Vecchio/Duomo, Florence II
566. Palomar Observatory, Mt. Palomar, Calif. II
567. Pan Am Building, New York, N.Y. IV
568. Pantheon, Rome IV *
569. Paris Cityscape, France IV *
570. Park Row Building, New York, N.Y. II
571. Parliament Building, Prague, Czech Republic IV
572. Parthenon, Athens, Greece IV *
573. Passau, Germany IV
574. Peace Arch, Blaine, Wash. & Douglas, B.C., Canada IV
575. Peninsular Life Insurance Company, Raleigh, N.C. III

576. Penn Mutual Life Insurance Company, Philadelphia IV
577. Pennsylvania State Capitol, Harrisburg, Pa. III
578. People's United States Bank, St. Louis, Mo. IV *
579. Peoria Statue, Ill. IV
580. Peterborough Cathedral, England II
581. Petersburg Mutual Savings, Va. III
582. Piaget Building, New York, N.Y. IV
583. Pierce National Life Insurance, Los Angeles II
584. Pilgrim Memorial Monument, Provincetown, Mass. II
585. Pink House, Wellsville, N.Y. IV
586. Pittsburgh Hilton and Towers, Pa. I
587. Plaza de Toros, Madrid, Spain II
588. Plaza Hotel, New York, N.Y. IV
589. Plymouth Plantation, Mass. III
590. PNB Tower, Philadelphia IV
591. Point Loma Lighthouse, Calif. III
592. Port Angeles Savings and Loan Association, Wash. III
593. Porta Nigra, Trier, Germany III
594. Portland Federal Savings, Oregon I
595. Posen Tower, Germany IV
596. Post Office Tower, London IV
597. Preferred Life Assurance Company, Montgomery, Ala. III
598. Pro Football Hall of Fame, Canton, Ohio II
599. Provident Savings Bank, Baltimore IV
600. Prudential Building, Boston IV
601. Prudential Building, Chicago III
602. Prudential Center, Boston IV
603. Pullman Bank and Trust, Chicago II
604. Pullman Trust and Savings Bank, Chicago IV
605. Pyramid, Giza, Egypt II *
606. Pyramid di Cais Cestius, Rome IV
607. Ralston Steel Corporation, Skokie, Ill. IV

608. RCA Building, New York, N.Y. III *
609. Regensburg Dom, Germany IV
610. Reid Library, Lake Forest College, Ill. IV
611. Reims Cathedral, France II
612. Rialto Bridge, Venice III
613. Ripon Cathedral, England III
614. Riverside National Bank, Ill. III
615. R.L.D.S. Auditorium, Independence, Mo. IV
616. Rochester Savings Bank, Rochester, N.Y. III
617. Rock Island Savings Bank, Rock Island, Ill. IV *
618. Roosevelt's Little White House, Warm Springs, Ga. III
619. Rose Bowl, Pasadena, Calif. III
620. Roskilde Domkirke, Denmark IV
621. Round Tower, Ireland IV
622. Royal Exchange Assurance, London III *
623. Royal Gorge, Colo. II
624. Royal Observatory, Copenhagen, Denmark IV
625. R.T. Crane Brass & Bell Foundry, Chicago II
626. Russell National Bank, Kans. IV
627. Rutherford County Courthouse, Tenn. III
628. Rutledge Tavern, New Salem, Ill. III
629. Sagrada Familia, Barcelona II
630. Saint Luke's Tower, Evanston, Ill. IV
631. Salem Federal Savings and Loan, Oreg. III
632. San Antonio, Padova, Italy IV
633. San Francisco Cityscape, Calif. II
634. San Jacinto Monument, Houston, Tex. II
635. San Joaquin Bank, Bakersfield, Calif. III
636. Santa Casa di Loreto, Italy IV
637. Santa Maria Della Salute, Venice IV
638. Santa Rosa Savings and Loan Association, Calif. II
639. Santa's Workshop, North Pole, N.Y. III
640. Schloss Stolzenfels, Germany IV *
641. Schrepenheuvel de Basiliek, Belgium III

642. S. Corazon-Tibidabo, Barcelona III
643. Scotiabank, Canada III
644. Scottish Rite Temple, Guthrie, Okla. IV
645. Scottish Rite Temple, Indianapolis III *

**Scottish Rite Temple, Indi-
anapolis, Indiana; lead, ca. 1940**

646. Scotty's Original Castle, Death Valley,
     Calif. III
647. Seagram Tower, Niagara Falls, N.Y. III
648. Sears Roebuck and Company, Chicago V
649. Sears Tower, Chicago II
650. Seattle Space Needle, Wash. I
651. Second National Bank, Houston, Tex. III
652. Second National Bank of Nashua, N.H. III
653. Second Ward Savings Bank, Milwaukee,
     Wis. III
654. Security Bank of Chicago V
655. Security National Bank, Joplin, Mo. III
656. Security Peoples Trust Company, U.S. IV
657. Security Trust Company, Lynn, Mass. V *
658. Seoul Main Stadium, Korea III
659. Serial Federal Savings and Loan Association,
     New York, N.Y. III

660. Shakespeare's Birthplace, Stratford-on-Avon,
     England III
661. Sharebuilders Federal Credit Union, U.S. III
662. Shasta Dam, Lake Shasta, Calif. V
663. Shea Stadium, New York, N.Y. IV
664. Shedd Aquarium, Chicago III
665. Shore Temple, Mamallapurum, India IV
666. Singing Tower/Bok Tower, Lake Wales, Fla. II
667. Skylon Tower, Niagara Falls, N.Y. II
668. Sleeping Beauty's Castle, Disneyland, Ana-
     heim, Calif. III
669. Sleeping Beauty's Castle, Magic Kingdom,
     Orlando, Fla. III
670. Smith Infirmary, Staten Island Hospital,
     N.Y. V
671. Smithsonian Institution, Washington, D.C. IV
672. Smith Tower, Seattle, Wash. IV
673. Snoopy's Dog House I
674. Soldiers and Sailors Monument, Indianapolis,
     Ind. III *

**Soldiers and
Sailors Monument,
Indianapolis,
Indiana; lead, ca.
1930**

675. South Dakota State University Campanile, Brookings, S. Dak. IV
676. Southern Methodist University, Dallas, Tex. IV
677. South Main State Bank, Houston, Tex. IV
678. Spaceship Earth, Epcot Center, Orlando, Fla. II
679. Spasakaya Tower, Kremlin, Moscow III
680. Speyer Dom, Germany IV
681. Sphinx, Giza, Egypt II
682. Split Rock Lightouse, North Shore, Minn. IV
683. St. Anne de Beaupre, Quebec, Canada II
684. St. Anne d'Ouvray, France V
685. St. Augustine Bridge, Fla. II
686. St. Augustine City Gate, Fla. I
687. St. Basil's, Moscow III *
688. St. Francis, Assisi, Italy IV
689. St. Joseph's Oratory, Montreal, Canada III *
690. St. Louis Cathredral, New Orleans IV
691. St. Louis Climatron, Mo. IV
692. St. Mark's/Campanile, Venice III
693. St. Mary's Cathredral/Giotto's Tower, Florence III
694. St. Mary's In the Mountains, Virginia City, Nev. IV
695. St. Michael's, Charleston, S.C. V
696. St. Patrick's, New York, N.Y. II
697. St. Paul Federal Savings of Chicago II
698. St. Paul's Cathedral, London III
699. St. Paul's Evangelical Lutheran Church, Fort Wayne, Ind. IV
700. St. Peter's, Rome II *
701. St. Peter's Church, Chicago III
702. St. Stephen's, Vienna, Austria IV
703. St. Stephen's Evangelical Lutheran Church, Chicago IV
704. State of Texas Building, Dallas, Tex. V
705. Statue of Liberty, New York, N.Y. I *
706. Steeple Building, Bishop Hill Colony, Henry County, Ill. III
707. Stockholm City Hall, Sweden II
708. Stockton Savings and Loan Society, Calif. IV *
709. Strasbourg Cathredral, France III
710. Straus National Bank and Trust Company, Chicago III
711. Sulgrave Manor, Northamptonshire, England III
712. Sunsphere, Knoxville, Tenn. II
713. Sun Tower, San Francisco II
714. Sydney Harbor Bridge, Australia II
715. Sydney Opera House, Australia III
716. Sydney Tower, Australia II
717. Syracuse Savings Bank, N.Y. III
718. Taj Mahal, Agra, India III
719. Tallahassee Federal Savings, Fla. III
720. Tarantino's Restaurant, San Francisco V
721. Tecumseh Monument, U.S. Naval Academy Annapolis, Md. III
722. Telephone Exchange, Chinatown, San Francisco, Calif. IV
723. Temple Bar, London IV *
724. Temple of Castor and Pollux, Rome III
725. Temple of Isis, Egypt IV *
726. Temple of Saturn, Rome III
727. Temple of Vesta, Rome IV *
728. Terminal Tower, Cleveland, Ohio III
729. Texas Bank, Dallas, Tex. III
730. Texas Stadium, Irving, Tex. III
731. Thunderbird Bank, Ariz. III
732. Timberline Lodge, Mt. Hood, Oreg. III
733. Tokyo Tower, Japan II
734. Tomb of Scipio, Rome IV *
735. Tonsberg Tower, Norway IV
736. Toronto City Hall, Canada III

737. Toronto Skyline, Canada III
738. Torre Assinelli, Bologna, Italy III
739. Torre de Belem, Portugal IV
740. Torre del Oro, Seville II
741. Torre Latino Americano, Mexico City, Mexico III
742. Totem Pole, Pioneer Square, Seattle, Wash. III
743. Tower Bridge, London II
744. Tower Federal Savings, Western Spring, Ill II
745. Tower of Jewels, San Francisco V *
746. Tower of Memories, Memorial Park, Whitemarsh, Montgomery County, Pa. IV
747. Tower of the Americas, San Antonio, Tex. III
748. Tower of the Masonic Peace Memorial, London IV *
749. Town Hall, Pozanan, Poland IV
750. Town Hall, Prague II
751. Traders Bank, Toronto, Canada IV *
752. Transamerica Pyramid, San Francisco IV *
753. Travel and Transportation Building, Chicago III *

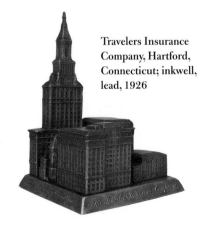

Travelers Insurance Company, Hartford, Connecticut; inkwell, lead, 1926

754. Travelers Insurance Company, Hartford, Conn. IV *
755. Trier Dom, Germany IV
756. Troitskoya Tower, Kremlin, Moscow III
757. Trondheims Domkirke, Norway IV
758. Trout Hall, Allentown, Pa. III
759. Trylon and Perisphere, 1939 World's Fair, N.Y. II *
760. Tufts College Chapel, Somerville, Mass. IV
761. Ulm Munster, Germany III
762. Union Dime Savings Bank, N.Y. IV
763. Union Easton Trust Company, St. Louis, Mo. V
764. Union Station, Los Angeles IV
765. Union Station, St. Louis, Mo. IV *
766. Unisphere, 1965 World's Fair, New York, N.Y. II
767. United American Bank, U.S. III
768. United Banking and Trust Co., U.S. IV
769. United Nations, New York, N.Y. II
770. United Savings and Loan Association III
771. University of Pennsylvania Stadium, Philadelphia III
772. University State Bank, Houston, Tex. III
773. URSS Exhibit, 1937 Paris Exposition, France V
774. USA Pavilion, 1958 Exposition Universelle Bruxelles, Belgium V *
775. U.S. Capitol, Washington, D.C. I
776. U.S. Fidelity and Guaranty Company, Baltimore III *
777. U.S. Supreme Court, Washington, D.C. IV *
778. Vanadium Building, Pittsburgh, Pa. IV *
779. Van Wickle Library, Layfayette College, Easton, Pa. IV
780. Venice column with animal, Venice IV
781. Venice column with figure, Venice IV

782. Victor Emmanuel Monument, Rome II *
783. Victory Monument, Berlin IV
784. Voice of South Australia V
785. Volkerschlaght Denkmal, Leipzig, Germany III
786. V. Satui Winery, St. Helena, Calif. II
787. Vulcan Monument, Birmingham, Ala. II
788. Waltham Federal, Waltham, Mass. III
789. Warner Brothers Studio Water Tower, Burbank, Calif. IV
790. Washington, D.C. Cityscape III *
791. Washington Mansion, Mt. Vernon, Va. III
792. Washington Monument, Washington, D.C. I
793. Washington's Headquarters, Valley Forge, Pa. III
794. Watchtower and Kiva, Grand Canyon, Ariz. III
795. Waterbury National Bank, Waterbury, Conn. III
796. Water Tower, Chicago II
797. Wausau Train Station, Wis. IV
798. Wells Cathedral, England III
799. Western Maryland Station Center, Cumberland, Md. III
800. Westin Bonaventure, Los Angeles I
801. Westminster Abbey, London III
802. Westside Presbyterian Church, Germantown, Pa. III
803. WFAA and KGKO Penthouse Studios, Dallas, Tex. III
804. White Heron Castle, Himeji, Japan II
805. White House, Washington, D.C. I
806. White Owl Cigar Exhibit, 1939 World's Fair, New York, N.Y. V *
807. Wichita Federal Savings and Loan Association, Kans. II
808. Wilderness Church, Silver Dollar City, Mo. IV
809. Wilhelm Dem Grossen Monument, Coblenz, Germany III
810. Will County National Bank, Joliet, Ill. V
811. Williamsburg Savings Bank, Pa. II
812. Will Rogers Shrine of the Sun, Colorado Springs II
813. Wilmington Mutual Savings and Loan, Calif. III
814. Wilton National Bank, U.S. V
815. Winnetka Trust and Savings Bank, Ill. III
816. Wisconsin State Capitol, Madison, Wis. II
817. Women's Christian Temperance Union, Chicago IV *
818. Wonder Wall, 1984 World's Fair, New Orleans III
819. Woolworth Building, New York, N.Y. II *
820. Worcester County Institution for Savings, Mass. III *
821. Worcester Federal Savings, Mass. II
822. Worcester Federal Savings, Springfield, Mass. II
823. World Trade Center, New York, N.Y. II
824. Wright Brothers National Memorial, Kitty Hawk, N.C. IV
825. Wrightsville Memorial, Pa. V
826. Wrigley Building, Chicago III *
827. Wurzburg, Germany IV
828. Wurzburg of Grand Rapids, Mich. III
829. Yale Bowl, New Haven, Conn. IV
830. Yarn Market, Dunster, England IV
831. Ye Olde Curiositie Shop, London II
832. Yomemon Gate, Nikko, Japan III
833. York Hall, U.S. V
834. Zagreb Cityscape, Yugoslavia IV
835. Zembo Mosque, Harrisburg, Pa. III

1000 Thanks

While assembling the Ace Architect collection of souvenir buildings has involved singlemindedness and devotion (we prefer these words to "obsession"), it has also been, like all large architectural projects, a thoroughly collaborative undertaking.

Especially appreciated is the encouragement of other collectors held in thrall to souvenir buildings, including Paul Alley, David Bond, Dort Brown, Jim Darr, Jim Elkind, Helen and Joe Grinton, Al Goldstein, Marty Gutierrez, Jamie Kessler, Randy Klinger, Dave Lynaugh, Chris Rickles, Dixie and Bill Trainer, and Anthony Tremblay.

We are continually surprised at the help and kind words offered by those who do not collect souvenir buildings, but share our admiration for miniature places, including S. Benedetti, Terry Bissell, Elsa Cameron, Renato Convalle, Ken Coupland, Don Duer, Susan Evans, Tom Kellogg, Howard Miller, Avram Roitman, and Barbara Thornburg.

Without souvenir buildings, the collection would not come to much. We are fortunate beyond fortunate that many resourceful people, almost all now friends, have contributed beyond reason to building the collection. Thank you Arline and Andy Anderson, Marie Bennett, Frank Briola, Susan and Bob Call, Larry Carey, Marilyn Cehelnik, Dennis Clark, Steve and Tony Conti, Doc and the Magic Lady, Frank Denski, Robert Descarpentris, George Fujimoto, Helene Guarnaccia, Ted and Lu Johns, Sandra Kaplan, Donal Markey, Dave and Julie Meyer, Margaret and Andrew Moore, Bob Pierce, Sandra Pitman, John Riccardelli, "Hey Pal" Russell, Jim Schultz, Esther and Gorden Schroff, Thomas Sept, Dan Toepher, Victoria Weyandt, and Neville Whittle.

Le Corbusier wrote that "Creation is a patient search." In fact, compared to assembling the most modest book, creation is a snap. Through the rigors of this project we have enjoyed the unaccountably unflagging assistance of George Beylerian, Darilyn Carnes, Jarrell Conner, Paul Goldberger, Alan Hess, Alec Iacono, Lucia and Max Howard, Judith Ogus, Ruth Peltason, and Alan Weintraub. To all of you, as always, 1,000 thanks.

Margaret Majua
David Weingarten